Enter into My Rest

The Mysteries of Living and Dying Revealed

Dear John,
Nicole and
Arlo! It was so
wonderful to see you!!!
with Love!
John Fubbs

Our Divinity by Lori Dobberstein (acrylic, 24 x 24)

Enter Into My Rest

The Mysteries of Living and Dying Revealed

By John Thomas Fuhler

Illustrations by Lori Dobberstein

Henschel
HAUS
publishing, inc.

Milwaukee, Wisconsin

Illustrations by Lori Dobberstein
Author photo by JonathansPortraits.com
Photos of Temple Mount by Pastor Eric Meyer, MDiv
Additional photos by the author.

Published by
HenschelHAUS Publishing, Inc.
Milwaukee, Wisconsin
www.henschelHAUSbooks.com

ISBN: 978159598-753-2
E-ISBN: 978159598-754-9
Audio ISBN: 978159598-755-6
LCCN: 2020934286

Dedication

To all of you who are given to me, whom I love very dearly.

CONTENTS

PREFACE

What is the purpose of a modern apocalypse, and why would you want to read it? Perhaps the most relevant argument is that you will die. As such, you might want to know what that means. But this effort is much more than a description of the experience of death and dying. For example, the ancient wisdom comprising the framework of these stories is metaphysical in nature. It behooves modern physicists to become familiar with the ideas of the most brilliant minds of those times.

At least on occasion the modern reader might find s/he agrees with the metaphysicians and mystics of times past in ways that few of us could imagine. If the reader happens to be descended from one of the Indian tribes of North America, it will be relevant that incorporated into these stories are never before documented revelations of Native genius. Though Europeans nearly eradicated that wisdom, the great Native leaders preserved that information in ways that have defied destruction. Theirs is a genius that cannot be ignored.

If you happen to be one of the many Jews and Christians harmoniously working on the reconstruction of the Temple, this book contains important concepts and relationships that must be understood before the first foundation stone can be set in place. The Temple was not just a house. And of course, the underlying premise of the book is the process of sanctification by

Enter into My Rest

which we are drawn closer to God. And that brings us back to the first point herein: *All of us will die.* The stories included in this book give glimpses of the glories that can be ours when we depart this mortal coil. Instead of facing life with fear and trepidation, we can be confident, joyous, willing participants in one of God's greatest gifts to humanity!

The following is a partial list of some whose guidance and input have contributed in some fashion to this work: Jonathan Ben Dov, Elizabeth Benchley, Bill Iseminger, John E. Clark, Cindy Bloom, Curly Bear Wagner, Paul Red Elk, Larry Kenosha, Rogers Clinch, Jim Marshall and Harold Williams; Richard H. and Carol J. Fuhler, Greg and Jean Wilde, Carl and Lynda Colby, Sandie Neitzel, Lori Dobberstein, Eric Meyer, Klaus Witz, Angelica Urquizo, Kira Henschel, Chris Kringel, and Bill and Madeleine Schwarz. In addition, I am very grateful to Mark Concannon, Elizabeth Gallagher, Jonathan Roob, and Eunice Fuhler for their creative inputs. A very special thank you to Adam Russel Britt for the numerous, ad hoc tutorials on digital media and information technology. There are many others, as well. To them all I am exceedingly grateful.

INTRODUCTION

In *The Hitchhiker's Guide to the Galaxy*, Arthur Dent poses this question to the Creators, who are about to extract his brain in order to learn the question for which the answer is forty-two, "How many roads must a man walk down..." Douglas Adams said it was only a joke and completely random. What if I told you that Arthur Dent's response is absolutely true?

I Corinthians 10:6 provides a direct allusion to the forty-two stage process, where it says, "These (events in the wilderness) become for us types (as it were), to the end that we will not be desirous of evil things, just as that lot desired." Here Paul is referring to the forty-two stage journey of the Israelites through the desert during the Exodus out of Egypt. The forty-two-stage journey provides a template for an individual's process of becoming whole. As it says, God was testing them to know what was in their hearts.

The synopsis is given in Numbers 33, but allusions to this process occur in several other places in the Bible. Matthew, writing to his Jewish brethren, lists forty-two generations from Abraham to Jesus in the first chapter of his gospel. The list is contrived. It is incomplete in regard to the genealogies in I-II Kings, and inconsistent with the genealogies given in Luke. One of the generations isn't even a person. The obvious question is, "Why?" The answer is that Matthew is clearly alluding to something else. That something is the forty-two stage wilderness journey. Not only did Matthew imply that Jesus is the fulfillment of God's command to Abram, "(You) go to yourself!", but he adds a subtle and absolutely satisfying touch, as well. Each of the forty-two generations is reckoned as forty-two years long, yielding the exact number of years between Abram's call out of Chaldea and Jesus' immersion by John in the Jordan!

Another allusion is found in the Apocalypse of John, where he equates Daniel's "time, times and a half" with forty-two months of thirty days each, or 1260 days. Using a classical literary device called a chiasm, John draws his reader's attention to both the forty-two stage process and its reward. The crux of the chiasm is given in Revelation 11:15 – 19:

> The kingdom of the world becomes the Lord's and his Messiah's
> The dead are judged
> Those destroying the earth will be destroyed
> God's heavenly temple is opened
> and
> The Ark of the Covenant appears

Here John states unequivocally that the culmination of the process is the inauguration of the Messianic Kingdom, equating it to the entry into the Promised Land in Numbers 33 and the advent of Messiah in Matthew 1.

This book of stories is not a detailed description or interpretation of the forty-two-stage journey of self-cultivation. Such things have been around at least twenty centuries and are readily available online. Rather, this is an anthology of forty-two experiences, people, ideas, dreams, and visions that have influenced my spiritual growth. I am a storyteller, not a theologian. I have never belonged to any organized religion. Undoubtedly one or more of these stories will be perceived as controversial, offensive, or heretical. But these are stories, as they happened. This book is not intended to be read as narrative prose, though the contents are more or less chronological. Some of the stories are actual emails written to friends. Others are portions of projects written for other purposes. Most of these stories have been shared with a friend or two over a cup of tea or a glass of wine. All are intended to inspire and uplift.

And if I can bring comfort to anyone contemplating suicide or someone who is completely overwhelmed by the world we live in, then I shall have succeeded. I struggled with suicidal depression from the age of thirteen. I learned at the age of thirty-six that I had mercury poisoning. It was a relief to know that there was a reason for the depression: I was in the top thirty-five percent of people poisoned by mercury! The process of removing the mercury from my system was arduous. But the benefits are wonderful. Again, if you are suicidal, whatever the cause, get help!

NOTE TO THE READER

I have strived to convey both a narrative of actual events, as well as thoughts, feelings, and otherworldly experiences associated with those events. In order to provide visual clues to my inner state of mind, or actual dreams taken from my journals, out-of-body and near-death experiences, and actual visions and prophesies, I have used italics rather than the standard Roman font.

The following two pages present the 16 layers of Lori Dobberstein's incredible, intuitive artwork that serve to enhance this story.

Enter into My Rest

Descriptions of the layered in-process artwork in *Our Divinity* by Lori Dobberstein.

1. Blessing/Intention for the Journey. The Individual representing all of us on the Earthly Spiritual path.

2. Pure of heart, One enters the Temple. The Journey begins .

3. Contemplating the Mount of Olives and surrounded by inspiration, education and miracles within the Temple, deep connection with Life is experienced. Realization of the inner and outer as one.

4. The Seed of Life holding the unlimited potential of creation is activated within

5. Women's Court. Women in a circle holding hands symbolizing the equal power of all women in this space to contribute and uplift.

6. Songs of Joy sung in the Women's Court initiates the powerful energy of Reverence

7. Porch of the Holy Place. Palm fronds symbolizing the Garden of Eden and roses symbolizing the Love and Grace of Mother Mary (Divine Feminine).

8. Veil of Second Temple. Moon phases symbolizing all that is mystical in the heavens and living within the earthly structure of time and space, earth's forces and laws of nature.

9. Constellations as our threshold to the cosmic realm.

10. Holy of Holies. Singing cherubim surround the Throne with faces of the lion, ox, human and eagle.

11. The Tree of Life within us is remade. One is now a bridge to Heaven on Earth.

12. Figure of Light Violet: the Individual transformed.

13. Pyramid: vehicle of transformation

14. Union of pyramid (Spirit) and inverted pyramid (Matter) creates Diamond of Perfection.* We are and always have been whole and complete.

(described in The Heart of "I AM" the Point of Divine Origin, by Robyn Mary Edward)

15. Flowering of Tree of Life and radiance of True Self within the Light of Source God.

16. Realization of Our Divinity and Unity with All That Is.

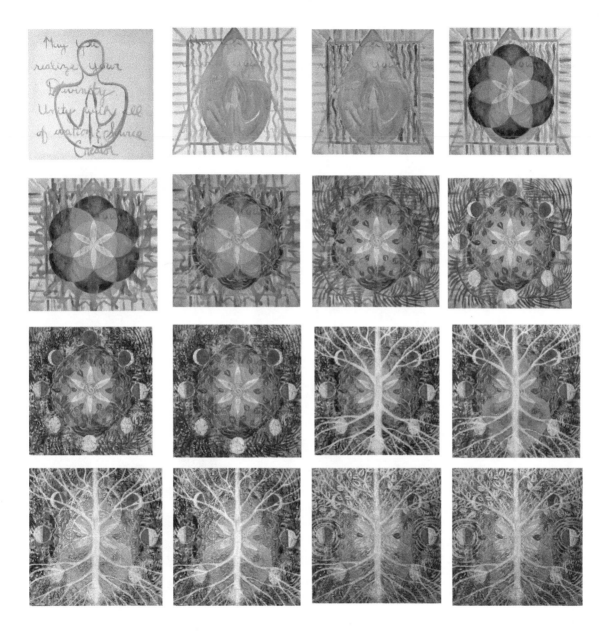

9   Enter into My Rest

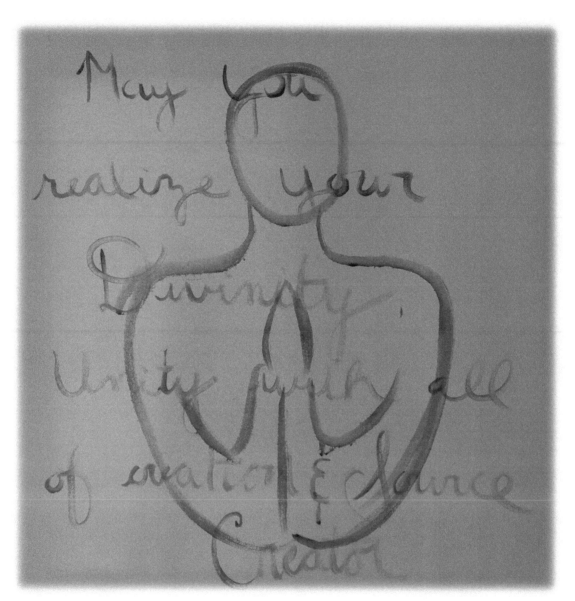

Our Divinity, layer 1

PART ONE
SEEKING GOD:
THE JOURNEY BEGINS

My maternal great-grandfather
and grandfather

My paternal grandmother

1

I AM

Curly Bear Wagner once told me, that it was the convention among the tribes of his area for a person to tell her/his audience who s/he was. In this way speakers provided their listeners with a context for understanding their perspective. So out of respect to that teaching...

I was born September 12, 1958 at 2:30 p.m. Central Daylight Savings Time in DeKalb, Illinois.

From the point of view of biology, I am of Saxon, Frisian, Bohemian, Irish, English, and Wyandot ancestry. Somewhere along the way Mongolian blood entered the stream on my father's side.

From the point of view of intellect my gifts lie in the areas of linguistics and mathematics. Human relations have always been important to me, so I have studied: English, Castilian and Mexican Spanish, High German, Classical and Koiné Greek, Hebrew and Latin. I have also formally studied Standard Levantine Arabic and Mandarin. Informally I have studied Sanskrit, Aramaic, Egyptian, Coptic, various Algonquian languages and French.

From the spiritual perspective I have studied Hinduism; Mahayana Buddhism, Tibetan Buddhism, and a little Zen; Rabbinic Judaism, Chasidism, and Kabbalah; Roman Catholicism, Evangelical and Southern Baptist Christianity, and Methodism; Messianic Judaism; Sufism; Zoroastrianism; Sikhism; and Egyptian, Cherokee, Anishinaabe and Lakota mysticism.

I've had more than fifty different addresses in California, Hawaii, Illinois, New Jersey, New York, Oregon, Virginia, and Wisconsin, as well as in Glasgow, Scotland. I've been homeless on multiple occasions in several locales. But my favorite residence was in the ancient Douglas fir forest of the Kalmiopsis Wilderness in the Siskiyou National Forest.

My favorite memories are living in *The Last of the Mohicans* country in the shadow of West Mountain. We could see the Green Mountains of Vermont from our backyard and our house was only a few minutes south of Lake George. It was an idyllic place for a child.

Several years my family and I lived just off a channel between Scull Bay and the Great Egg Harbor in New Jersey. Most summer days we lived on the beach, digging sand crabs or clams, finding starfish, and avoiding jelly fish. At first, it was like a dream...

2

ALL SADHUS OUT OF THE CAVES

By nature, I am an introvert. I have been content to be alone for extended periods of time. When I was young, I cultivated great disdain for human beings, much as Jonah nurtured hatred of the Ninevites. There was no motivation to seek companionship.

Instead, I filled my days with traveling the United States, reading the Bible, contemplating reality, praying, and singing sacred songs. I lived on the West Coast when I could. I had neither debt nor obligations except the immediate demands of the body.

It isn't as if my life became one long and continuous communion with the Divine. In fact, my life has been, if anything, ordinary, consisting of mundane jobs, daily routines, rent, bills, feeding the body, and so on. Ordinary, but punctuated by what Maslow called "peak experiences." The first awakening was experienced seventeen residences, twenty years, and 20,000 miles after my birth.

3

DEATH IN ARGYLL

...But me and my true love will never meet again
on the bonnie, bonnie banks o' Loch Lomond...
—Traditional Scottish Song

Death in reality is quite different from Hollywood dramatizations. There the producers and directors depend on emotional stimulation and gore to achieve their goal of financial gain. No, death can be, well, mundane. However, there are aspects of death and dying that are anything but mundane.

My year abroad was spent in Glasgow at the university. It is the fourth oldest university in Britain and the second oldest in Scotland. My course of study included archaeology, fine art and medieval history. My archaeology professor, Leslie Alcock, was world famous for his work on King Arthur's Cadbury-Camelot. He'd been Sir Mortimer Wheeler's deputy during the excavation of Mohenjo Daro in what is now Pakistan. During World War II he served in the British Army. He was tough but forgiving.

One of the great benefits of his class for a foreign exchange student was regular field trips to archaeological sites, such as Bronze Age and Iron Age hill

A section of the Antonine Wall in Scotland

Inside Edinburgh Castle

forts, Roman garrisons along the Antonine Wall, Romanesque and Medieval churches and cathedrals, and of course, Edinburgh Castle.

One such trip was to see the Nether Largie Cairns and a stone circle near Kilmartin Glen in Argyllshire. It started out beautifully. My friend and I took the front seats. For me it was like a free guided tour of Kilmartin by way of Loch Lomond. The front window of the coach extended from the floor to the ceiling, like a big screen TV. I was thrilled at the opportunity to see country-side that I would otherwise never have had the chance to see.

North of Paisley and just off the lake shore we were going around an s-curve. The hedged in road was designed for buggies, it was that narrow. Certainly, it was not designed to accommodate both large touring coaches and

Enter into My Rest

little white Toyotas carrying four teens ditching school, drinking wine and traveling at high rates of speed on the wrong side of the road.

I'd never actually seen death. Only once had I been to a wake, and that was for someone I'd never even met. That was about to change.

I don't know if what happened was the result of my hangover from my indulgences with my best friend the previous evening. And no amount of tobacco or that powdered instant beverage they pass off as coffee could remove the alcohol from my blood. Perhaps the residual alcohol loosened my soul from my body.

I saw the sudden shock of the realization of their peril in the faces of those four children, two guys in front and two girls in back. The driver was a beautiful, dark-haired man of seventeen, and the front seat passenger his ruddy redheaded friend. The driver was dead before the Toyota ground to a halt.

I turned my head so as not to see the impact. And then we crashed. I shot out of my forehead

as time stretched into eternity
...into the field,
through the hedgerow,
over the bushes and rocks...

Wait a minute! I know this place, I thought to myself. Whereas this was a completely novel experience to my adult mind, while out in that field I remembered the last time I'd experienced that consciously. It was now as if I were in three places: the student on the field trip, the spirit out in the middle of the field, and the holographic memory of my childhood, all happening simultaneously.

The last time I'd been in that space was when I was still a child, when we moved from Normal, Illinois to Atlantic City, New Jersey. My dad had accepted a promotion to an administrative position after having taught at the university. We were eastbound on the Pennsylvania Turnpike smack dab in the middle of an Appalachian blizzard! The turnpike was closed, and we had to spend the night in a rather quaint, old-fashioned hotel located in a little ski-town in Maryland. In that Loch Lomond out-of-body moment, I remembered having been able to enter that dimension at will, as I witnessed my little boy astral body walking around that suite of rooms.

And then suddenly, instantly, I was back in my body. It had only been the blink of an eye in real time. The Toyota had turned ninety degrees as it scraped against the coach, not stopping until it was halfway down its length. The professor and the two TAs ran to assist the injured children. Caught up in the drama of the moment, David and I followed them. Whereas they ran to help the Toyota's passengers, we smoked a cigarette. We were worse than useless...

Eventually I returned to the coach, walked to its middle and looked at that face of death. There in the front seat was the corpse of the driver. His skin was grey-blue from the lack of blood. His eyes were open, but the light had gone out. The left cornea was cracked as if made of glass. There was only a small trickle of blood at the corner of the mouth.

I saw the professor helping the ruddy redhead out of the front seat. The still semi-conscious lad screamed as they removed his body. This was not at all surprising as the engine was in his lap.

Somehow someone had phoned the police. *Why is this taking so long? What is the matter with this country? Are they coming all the way from Glasgow?* I was angry and frustrated. It took about a half hour for the police to

Enter into My Rest

arrive and even longer for the ambulances. Real time dragged on. The girls in the back of the bus were talking to relieve the tension. No one was crying. I suppose all of us were in shock.

The professor had a flask that he shared mercifully with the distressed bus driver and the ruddy youth. We waited there for a replacement touring coach to arrive. I thought it was to take us home. Only later would we discover that the professor intended to continue the field trip! *Is he out of his mind? How does he expect us to continue with this day? We haven't even had a chance to process the event, let alone prepare ourselves to jump right back into a field trip!* I was enraged and in shock. I had no context with which to understand the tragedy. My mother's death began a process, and this gave it urgency. Ultimately it exacerbated the suicidal tendencies that I had suffered since puberty.

Numbly we boarded the new coach and continued on our journey to Nether Largie Cairns.

4

I AM LOVE

Four residences, 8,000 miles and three years later I found myself home-less, alone, dejected, sick, depressed, penniless, unskilled, inexperi-enced, without guidance, without direction, without goals, not knowing the purpose of life, having no particular reason to live and no desires strong enough to motivate me. There I was in the rabbit warren called my friend's apartment. It was scarcely more than a bedroom. The communal bathroom was outside. A hotplate served as his kitchen.

My friend was in Mexico with his friend, so he allowed me to make use of his place while he was gone. I was trying to get my head together. Having been turned away by the head of the department on the grounds that I couldn't navigate the politics, and not having a backup plan, I found myself with a great big question mark staring me in the face!

When the opportunity had arisen to hitch a ride with a friend on his way to Berkeley, I jumped on it. He had a half '65, half '66 sea-blue Volkswagen Bug that struggled to hit 65 mph going downhill! It was a real adventure getting up the grade between Reno and Truckee! Luckily a couple of eighteen-wheelers were with us all the way. We'd pass them going uphill, and they'd pass us going down. It was an elegant *pas de trois* on wheels! Their presence was a comfort, as well as protection from the more aggressive drivers. I was relieved when we began the long descent down into Sacramento. That was in August 1981. It took only four short months for my life to fall apart completely.

I'd found a job almost immediately, doing archaeological excavations and surveys. It was a great way to see the state, get fresh air and exercise. But occurring as it did during the Recession, our customers—from big corporations to small property owners—couldn't afford to pay their contracts. Some even bartered!

So, there I was in the rabbit warren contemplating the flow of events that had led up to that point in time. In that very instant, the purest blue light filled my body and spoke, "I am love." In that instant, I comprehended the mechanics of the universe.

5

NOW I SEE YOU, NOW I DON'T

Six residences, 4,450 miles and eight months later, and technically homeless again, when I was a hippy and owned nothing but a change of clothes, a cigarette lighter and a Bible, when I was shuffling between the West Coast and Central Illinois, I had the great good fortune to meet a holy man.

I was staying with Harold and his family in their converted tool shed. Their three-story tent had only recently burned down because the canvas roof had caught fire. The local Rural Fire Protection District refused to allow it to burn to the ground, so the skeleton of charred posts, floorboards and two-by-fours stood like a sun-bleached corpse inhabited by scorpions and lizards.

Harold was my first teacher. As a child he used to race his brother up the side of the barn to see who would be the first to touch the weathervane. Of course, Harold won every time! By the time I met him, he had died multiple times. He also had the gift of healing by touch. He could teleport and levitate, and he could read minds. Harold also spoke with God.

Having grown up with Carlos Castaneda, it never occurred to me not to believe Harold. But magic, per se, never interested me. What I wanted was to bring healing to peoples' hearts, minds, and souls.

Enter into My Rest

One day, while listening to a recording of Harold reading his poetry, I heard him say, "I am love." These being the very words spoken to me by the voice in Albany, California, I just knew I had to meet him. And so, with the help of some friends I found myself in Cave Junction having apple pie with Harold at one of the local restaurants. And he invited me to come and stay with him and his family.

Every Wednesday night, Harold and his wife would convene a meditation followed by healing prayer. People came great distances to participate because Harold and his wife were such profound healers. My first time we participants included the neighbors, some townies, and a couple all the way from California. Among our group were a few Okies and Arkies who'd escaped the Depression-era dustbowl by homesteading the forest. I'd gotten high before the meditation, for no reason in particular but that someone had offered it.

Harold conducted a meditation that began with the heart, combining the life in the breath with the love in the blood and the Light of the Spirit. Then we visualized expanding that light to fill the stomach and the organs of digestion, then down the thighs and calves all the way to the soles of the feet. Then we visualized the energy of the earth combining with the love, light and life rising up the spine, ultimately coming to rest in the midbrain at the place behind the eyebrows, in the middle of the forehead. And then, after the forty-minute process concluded, Harold opened up the floor to prayer requests. Immediately one of the ladies present stated without apology that she would be first because she had injured her upper back badly and she was suffering tremendously.

I was at the age when young people are riddled with anxiety. So, in order not to interfere with the good vibes of the healing, I resolved to still my mind as much as conceivably possible under the circumstances. I closed my eyes and hoped to return to the meditation-induced alpha state.

As I sat there with my eyes closed, I saw someone's shadow walk across the room and stand behind the woman being healed. My mind interpreted this as Harold walking to the space behind her in order to make the healing more effective. So, being curious and not wanting to miss any of the show, I opened my eyes to watch.

What I saw blew my mind. There was nobody standing behind her or walking around the room! All attendees were in their original seats, with their eyes closed, and their hands folded in prayer, exactly as they had been. I closed my eyes again and saw that same shadow figure walk back to Harold's chair. Again, I opened my eyes and again there was no one walking around the room! Everyone was in the exact same chair as before. Afterward, when we were being debriefed, I shared this experience with the group. No one said a single word. And they all looked at me as if I had four heads!

That night I learned that Harold had the gift of leaving his body at will, and that I had the gift of sight.

6

MANNA FROM HEAVEN

A few weeks and a few miles later, and still homeless, I departed from Harold's home and set out for the Idaho Rainbow Gathering. It was very difficult to leave as Harold and his wife sang me a bon voyage prayer. I felt like crying, but I had 750 miles ahead of me. So, I buried my feelings and walked away without looking back.

I left Kerby that June morning and managed to score one ride to Grants Pass, a disappointing total of twenty-seven miles! My drivers were a couple of men supplementing their no doubt meager incomes with whatever scrap metal they could find on the side of the road. Their ambition and *joie de vivre* were disproportionately great for the modest earnings they achieved. But then, they were doing better than me! They dropped me off at the entrance ramp to the interstate.

Figuring it behooved me to get a jump on the next day's journey, I walked up Interstate 5 to the north side of Grants Pass. At first the weather was fine, but soon it began to drizzle. Then it turned into a good old Oregon deluge. Happily, I was near a rest stop. It was a modest cinder block structure without any refinements or frills. There wasn't even an overhang sufficient to provide shelter from the rain, so I hung out in the men's room till the rain cleared.

For the most part, none of the tourist families paid attention to me, in spite of my army surplus pants, bright red sweatshirt, rainbow suspenders, long hair, and untrimmed beard. Harold's wife had given me cans of tapioca and a brick of Velveeta from the local food pantry. The first I loved, but the second I hated almost more than anything else on the planet.

When the rain eventually stopped, I took my bedroll, consisting of a sheet of Visqueen and a pink blanket, and found a tree set back from the entrance ramp to the highway. I pitched a 'tent' and attempted to sleep. Attempted is the operant word, as the crack of hunting rifles continued well into the night, most likely the shots of hunters poaching game in the forest in order to feed their families.

The next morning, I was up with the sun. The rain had cleared out. The cool mountain air was bracing and beautiful. The mountains to the west were green with ancient forests and modern tree farms. The smell of wood smoke wafted from the chimneys of the cabins and homesteads that dotted the slopes adjacent the highway. Wisps of clouds driven by the distant ocean breeze brushed the peaks as they whispered sweet nothings to the forest trees. The pavement was still damp from the previous night's rains.

I'd already smoked my last cigarette and the nearest store was miles away! That's when the craving hit. I knew I was in sacred space and could have had anything I desired. Normally when I experienced that sacredness, I silenced my mind, lest I engender some unanticipated consequence. But the tobacco craving overpowered my will and I, addressing the Lord in my heart, said, "I could really use a cigarette." And I continued walking.

There, only a few paces ahead of me in the center of a dry patch of otherwise rain-drenched pavement was a lone menthol cigarette, dry as a bone. Now I hate menthol cigarettes. They dry my throat, they mask the

Enter into My Rest

wonderful flavor of the tobacco, and they cool the lungs. So, I passed up the cigarette.

Not ten yards up the road the craving returned. But, given the hundreds of miles remaining in my journey, it seemed really stupid to back track even a few yards for the sake of a smoke. So, I stayed the course and continued walking north.

And the craving returned with a vengeance.

I repeated this dance two more times. Finally, the voice said, "You really are a stupid man!" But, still not wanting to lose any time by backtracking, I chose to continue walking north. Once again, the craving returned. This time, however, I resolved not to pass up any gifts of tobacco. This time...

This time there was an unopened package of menthol cigarettes sealed in a cellophane wrapper, lying in a dry patch of otherwise soaking wet pavement! And I grabbed the whole pack!

Lesson learned! If God gives you quail, eat quail and be grateful! I guess that goes for Velveeta, too.

Our Divinity, layer 2

7

HERE I AM

"*and suddenly a light from heaven surrounded him...*" (Acts 9:3)

2,625 miles, one month and one residence later...

"All I ever wanted was to be happy." July 6, 1982, I witnessed the total eclipse of the moon from atop a mountain in western Idaho. I was living in the makeshift Visqueen and fir-branch tent. Truck-tire cords held the shelter together. Pale lavender St. Elmo's fire conducted by the truck-tire cords illuminated my tent when the lightning ionized the air. The incessant rain dripped in through the hole at the very peak of the tent. If I slept in a fetal position, the drops fell between my elbows and knees. Staphylococcus from the mountain soils infected my feet, which had been sawn open by the rasp-like truck-tire cords I had used to tie on the soles, which had melted away from the upper shoes on the blistering pavement outside Eugene, Oregon. And I had contracted amoebic dysentery from drinking improperly treated mountain water. In that moment, it really sucked to be me.

It had been an arduous adventure hitchhiking from southwest Oregon to west central Idaho. I'd camped beneath the Three Sisters, praying the bears would forgive me encroaching on their land near Bend, where I was stopped by a policeman who was searching for a murderer who'd been seen passing through. *I look like a murderer?* I in my rainbow second-hand clothing walked through a biker town in Idaho, and finally got a ride in an antique fire engine with a bunch of fashion-independent hippies heading to the same locale as I.

It was miserably cold just below the tree line. The creek water was so cold it took away my breath. At night we could see way down the Weiser River valley as it wound its way through several villages and towns. We were perched high above the valley across which we could see the Saw Tooth Mountain range. It rained incessantly, which wasn't surprising if you consider that half the time we were inside a cloud. I saw ball lightening in hues of pink and green and powder blue exploding all around. Who says ball lightning doesn't exist? The rain caused all the old logging roads to turn into deep troughs of slip, which is where I caught the staph infections.

After only one week, it was time for me to head home. I was too sick to hitchhike; and I needed immediate medical attention. I caught a ride to the Vista Avenue exit on Interstate 84 south of Boise. I phoned my dad from the Boise International Airport. "Can you buy me a ticket home?"

After some moments, "Where are you?"

"Boise, Idaho."

"What is the phone number you're calling from?"

It was a payphone in the airport. After a few short minutes he phoned again. "There is a bus terminal in downtown Boise. Can you get there?"

"Yes."

"There will be a ticket waiting for you at the terminal. There isn't a bus until tomorrow morning, so you'll have to find a place to spend the night. I'll wire you some money which you can pick up at the Western Union inside the bus terminal. Do you have any identification on you?"

"Yes." I had my passport on me.

It was already late in the day. I walked up the road leading to downtown Boise. Though I was completely unself-conscious about my appearance, I must have been quite the sight. When it became dark, I found myself a vacant lot with a lone weeping willow tree. I hid myself under the branches and fell into a restless, lonely sleep.

The brisk dawn air woke me. It was going to be a clear, sunny day—not a cloud in the sky. I was starving and dehydrated as I hadn't eaten food or drunk water since the previous morning. As I walked through the cold canyons of the vacant Boise business district, I prayed, "I need something to eat, God. I'm exhausted. I can't wait for the restaurants to open, I'm starving." I had to keep moving. I couldn't miss that bus.

There ahead of me on the sidewalk was a white paper bag. When I stood over it, I could see a standard-sized loaf of Italian bread inside. It was perfect in every way. I was absolutely the only one on the streets, not a person or vehicle in sight. The bread was unblemished. There were no wet spots, no ants or other insects, not even the tiniest speck of dust. I didn't have to think twice. This really was manna from Heaven. With a primal sort of gratitude, I ate every crumb.

I feel so awful. Six foot two and only 135 pounds.

"All I'm trying to do in this earth is to be as much love for everyone as I am able."

"Who do you think you are?"

Funny. I thought I was being the bare minimum of what we're supposed to be. Yuh know, John 15:12, 'This is my commandment, that you all love one another, as I have loved you.' The Bible. Am I the only one who takes this stuff seriously?

I can't abide this culture. I need to get away from here. I need to be with my friends. I need a safe environment.

My body bears the memory scars of childhood sexual abuse. Dr. Feinberg was no help. She wouldn't even have a cup of coffee with me. Shrinks! Why do I feel like such a loser when I'm doing what we're supposed to be doing?

"If you all love me, you all will keep my commandments." (John 14:15)

Memory of my mother's death. People whose mothers die while they are still children are said to be blessed. I was so thankful when she died. I want to feel bad about that, but I was so relieved the physical abuse was at an end. Regularly she used to beat me bloody. She couldn't control her temper. Can a child possibly be that bad?

She used to beat me so violently my head would ring, and I would tell my siblings that I was a robot.

I couldn't remember who sexually abused me. In fact, I can't remember some eighteen months of my life. All I know are the symptoms I exhibit. And the emptiness I feel. And the physical and emotional pain I suffer every waking moment of my life. All I want is to be happy. I don't know how to be happy.

My roommates were fighting over *tchotchkalas*. Here the world is about to implode from World War III, children are starving to death, or being beaten to death, or being sexually abused right next door, the earth is heading toward global environmental catastrophe, and they're arguing about trifles.

My Environmental Sciences professor had told us that if we stopped all the carbon emissions now it was already too late. My Political Science professors convinced me that politicians and lawyers were the problem. What happened to

Enter into My Rest

Government of the people, by the people, and for the people? Don't the people even care?

"CAN'T YOU JUST PRETEND YOU ARE FRIENDS?"

I have to get out of here.

> "I looked when he opened the sixth seal,
> and a great earthquake occurred,
> and the sun became black as sackcloth,
> and the whole moon became as blood..."
> (Revelation 6:12)

I thought I might be able to deduce the meaning of this verse by repeating it over and over and over: red like blood......................red like blood....................red like blood. What does this mean? July 6, 1982. Red like blood.

> "and the stars of heaven fell to the earth...
> because the great day of His anger has come,
> and who is able to stand?"
> (Revelation 6:17)

What time is it? Does anybody know what time it is? Is the day of wrath upon us? upon me? Where can I go for help? I desperately need to get away from here.

I had only been home a week and already I couldn't make it work. So, I decided to hitchhike to Plain City. My friends would be able to help me. It was a particularly muggy July day in the Land of the People. I headed south with only my shirt on my back. The air hung around me like a thick down parka.

On both sides of the road were the robust fields of corn that grace the Heartland. Birds were busily engaged in their routines as thunderheads accumulated in the sky. In the ditch beside the road were cattails in the prime of their season.

"The cattail roots are delicious eaten raw. Indian people will never go hungry because they know how to live off the land," my Chumash friend, Tom, had said.

Too bad I don't have a knife.

Along the way, I saw a church and the pastor's house adjacent to it. I was dehydrated and desperately needed water. When I walked around to the front door, I saw the family, consisting of the pastor, his wife, and their two pre-teen daughters, seated at the table for dinner. I knocked on the screen door, but no one even turned around. I knocked yet again, and again no one turned around even so much as to acknowledge me. The pastor was facing me through the screen door from about fifteen feet away. "Pretend he isn't there, and he'll go away."

Our Lord's words came to mind:

"I was thirsty, and you did not give me a drink..."
(Matthew 25:42)

A little farther up the road I saw an overweight man in Bermuda shorts and a tee-shirt in front of his orange, three-bedroom, clapboard ranch house. There were no trees or bushes to shield it from the highway and the probing eyes of passersby. I walked up to him and asked him for a drink. He told me to help myself to the hose, which I did thankfully. The water tasted like car oil and gasoline, but it quenched my thirst. I felt sorry for him for having to drink the run-off from the highway.

Enter into My Rest

It became late quickly, and I was losing hope. I'd been hitchhiking several hours with only one ride from a gay couple to show for my efforts. The physical pain, hunger, disillusionment, confusion and emotional agony were taking their toll.

Seventy-five percent of children who lose their mothers to death suffer depression. All too often it goes undetected.

It seemed I had nothing whatsoever to lose but the nonstop pain and emptiness I was suffering.

Dead mother never buried. She never even hugged me or told me she loved me. All I ever wanted was to go with her on a bike ride to the bay.

I had managed to cover thirty miles when I arrived in Speedtrap, population 2,000. The community had one church, five taverns, and one gas station. As I approached the tracks that divide the town in two, I heard the music from one of the bars. It was decorated with nauseating, bilious yellow lights. I couldn't go a step further. I hit rock bottom right there at the tracks in that notorious little community.

I'd been suicidal since puberty, at which time in my life hopelessness overtook me. Not that there weren't entertaining distractions. There were. Underlying the façade, however, were toxic levels of mind-clouding mercury, and the absence of a reason to endure this life. I had lived in such a way that I had done everything I could imagine doing. Perhaps I have limited imagination. And, not having been raised in the church, I felt no moral imperative not to commit suicide.

The Cold War was just winding down. In my "International Relations since 1950" class we had discussed the millions of people who would be mere collateral damage during a nuclear attack as if we were discussing going to Vegas for a weekend of indulgence.

Am I the only one who thinks this might be a little insane?

"If they suddenly announced the Russians had launched a nuclear missile attack targeting the Midwest, I would walk to the edge of town and watch the sunset." How many times had my friends and I discussed this possibility?

"You know Tricky Dick had his finger on the button one night during a drinking binge." I was already headed for a nervous breakdown by the time I graduated college.

Seventeen years of education and one college degree and I didn't even know how to take care of myself.

So, I was finished. I made the decision to end my life there in Speedtrap, USA. I had never actually thought about how I would do it, so I had to ponder this. I hadn't come prepared, as it were, although my life on the street had taught me how to think on my feet.

Unexpectedly, I heard a voice. It was Mary, the mother of Jesus.

"What would you feel if your youngest brother did this?" she asked.

She knew how much I loved him.

Knowing that there was nothing to lose and choosing to be as honest as I knew how, I answered, "I would be VERY angry."

"Why?"

Her question neutralized me completely. "Because I would know he wasn't seeing all the options available to him." She challenged me in that moment to find the options for my life that I couldn't see. My shoulders slumped. I would have to get back into the fight.

I spent the night beneath the rubber-link mud trap in the entrance vestibule of the local elementary school. The next morning one of the custodians gave me enough money to phone my dad, who sent my brothers to retrieve

Enter into My Rest

me. When I returned home, I phoned my best friend, Hieronymus. "I need to trip. Can you come today?"

It was a weekday and he was at work. "I can't come today, John. I have to work."

"Can you come on Saturday?"

"I can't. I have a wedding to go to. How about Sunday?"

So, Sunday it was. When he came over, we drove to a local forest preserve and he proceeded to feed me massive quantities of psilocybin mushrooms, which I consumed willingly. I really wasn't paying very close attention as I tried to explain to him what was happening inside. "The sun will become dark and the moon will become red like blood. I don't know what it means. It's as if something is missing and I don't know what it is." Neither of us knew how really ill I was, and the drugs had a far more potent-than-usual effect on me.

The intense July afternoon oozed into the future. Over and over I tried to integrate all the loose ends into a coherent whole. My mother's violence, her death, my roommates, my education, current world events, apparent environmental collapse, the incipient spirituality which I was attempting to live out, and now, Bible prophecy. I had no context for any of this. It overwhelmed me. On top of all this confusion were so many toxic emotions as well as my physical illness. I was a wreck inside and out. No Joy, no Love, no Peace. I was completely and utterly broken.

And then it happened. The Lord took me. I thought I was having a heart attack, so rapidly was it beating in my chest. The pain in my muscles and joints was excruciating. My roommates were arguing in the background while my friend looked anxiously into my eyes, "What's the matter?"

Purple-tipped arrows of Light pierced my mind as I was filled with his Presence. A voice as gentle as butterfly wing beats speaking out of my heart said, "Here I am." The Light of his Presence permeated everything around me. Everything was gone except for the body that appeared like crystals of every color of the rainbow, with purple circles of light surrounding the eyes. His Presence was my only remaining link between materiality and Spirit. The light was simultaneously rock solid, freezing cold and an all-consuming fire. Every pain I had ever known I experienced in that moment, and at the same time my eyes experienced the greatest pleasure possible. Everything was as if permeated by one solid block of living, frozen, eternal light.

In that short-lived epiphany I understood what I had been missing.

Not that I accepted it. Doesn't Exodus 33:20 say, "Certainly no man could be able to see my face and live."? Doesn't John 1:18 say, "No one has ever seen God."? And yet, there I was standing in pure, tangible, conscious Light.

Only seconds after it had begun, the Light was gone, the pain subsided, the Spirit withdrew, and I was restored to normal consciousness. I advised my friend how to brew a medicinal tea, which would facilitate the removal of the drugs from my system. I had to lie down to avoid passing out. My friend brought me the tea, which I drank quickly. Minutes later I was making a dinner of barbecued chicken and green beans.

It took months for me to process the experience for which I had no intellectual foundation. I'd had it in my mind that God was completely and utterly transcendent, and that only the truly, truly, truly worthy by virtue of their righteous behavior could ever hope to experience his Presence. And if anybody were unworthy it was I. My life since puberty had been spent breaking all 613 laws in the Old Testament. What I hadn't actually done I had thought about doing. I ought to have been stoned to death several times over. I struggled to reconcile my concept of a punishing God with this one who had spoken so kindly to me in my heart. I struggled with a God who in his Being never judged me. In that moment I resolved to deny myself and take up my cross and follow him.

> "For whoever wishes to save his life will lose it;
> but whoever loses his life for my sake will find it."
> (Matthew 16:25)

8

HOLY SPIRIT

One hundred and fifty miles, one residence and only a few weeks later...
After several weeks I was infused with the Holy Spirit. To say that I was convicted is an understatement! To say I was exposed would be inadequate to describe the absolutely all-encompassing invasion of my whole person with that force. On my path, I had focused on reforming my conduct. But I had overlooked the more meaningful matters. My sexual indiscretions were as nothing in comparison to the ugliness of my heart and my mouth. Up till that time I had found humor in the sufferings of others. All the disgust over the behavior of others, or their appearance, or their smell. Never had I felt so small. So very, very small. And of course, there was the disdain for human beings, for their inability to control their passions, appetites, alcohol consumption, and anger.

I would say that I was humiliated, but there was no practical advantage to indulging in that feeling. Nor self-hatred. Nor regret. It was way too late for that. My slate was blemished. I had made my bed. I was in the depths of the hell of my own making and there was only one way out. I had to change my mind and adjust my attitude.

9

MEETING JESUS

As you did it onto the least of these my siblings...
(Matthew 25:40)

Six months later, same residence...

Spring of 1983 marked the first time the Lord came to me in a dream. I'd been praying to see him, so desperately did I desire his presence.

Our Lord was sitting in a wheelchair. I was feeding him something with the texture of oatmeal, some of which dribbled from the corner of his mouth. Carefully I wiped his mouth, at which point he allowed me to gaze into his eyes, those steady, gray-blue eyes behind which the infinity of God's eternity shone calmly forth. I entered into the transcendent divinity beyond the face of the person and quickly lost self-awareness.

10

THE SCREAM

A month or two later, same residence...

The last years of her life found my mother becoming increasingly violent. My younger brother and I were the usual targets. Regularly she drew blood.

It hadn't always been so. In her twenties, my mother was very beautiful. She had the wonderful lips of her German ancestors, and the warm brown complexion, brown eyes and dark hair inherited from her Wyandot grandfather. She passed along the brown hair and skin to my only sister, who was mistaken for Navajo by her Indian co-workers.

And then came that night that changed all our lives forever. We children went to bed at dusk, when the whole world relaxed. The shadows of the trees' gently rustling leaves danced on our bamboo roll blinds. I pulled my blanket right up under my chin, so no evil being could get me while I slept.

That night was unexceptional in every way, until, that is, my mom died. I heard the whispers of Jack and his wife, co-workers of my dad, who'd driven all the way from Brigantine Island to stay the night. I heard the sirens whining into the distance, as they took my mother to the hospital in the community to the south.

Enter into My Rest

The next morning, my dad gathered us together to break the news. When he said our mom was dead, my heart breathed a big sigh of relief!

In June of 1982, while visiting Harold, I remembered experiencing my mother's soul take flight. It was rather like witnessing a holographic version of Edvard Munch's *The Scream*. Inasmuch as children are psychologically attached to their mothers, we all experienced her death. And she was terrified. Not only did I witness her death holographically, but I re-experienced that terror!

Once I was grieving the fact that my mother, who'd become so hard of heart, had never said, "I love you." As I customarily did before going to bed, I prayed. That night I petitioned God to take away that emptiness.

Early the next morning Ananda Mayi Ma visited me for the first time. There in my bedroom was her presence, as she filled me with golden light. This was not a yellow light or a metaphoric light. No, it was an all-pervasive, metallic-gold light. And my heart was filled with the joy of the knowledge of a mother's love. To this day, my heart tangibly softens when I look into her face!

Only one other time have I seen that metallic-gold light. That was while visiting one of the weeping icons at a church in the suburbs of Chicago. Looking on from the balcony, watching the relative chaos of the Orthodox Mass trying to drown out the din of the steady stream of pilgrim onlookers wanting to witness the tears, I noticed that the icon farthest on the left was radiating gold light. It was an image of the Holy Mother and not the weeping icon over which so much fuss was being made.

As none of my friends could see the way I do, I refrained from mentioning it. But when the opportunity arose to converse with one of my saint friends, I mentioned the phenomenon. She had seen the gold light emanating from the same icon, as well! Our Mother was blessing us all with the gold light of her presence, and we didn't even know it!

CALLING DOWN THE ALIENS

A few days and four hundred miles later, same residence...

One time, while walking from the parking lot at the 1983 Michigan Rainbow Gathering my friend and I met a couple men struggling to heave a Steinway piano up the ancient mountain to the prayer circle at the top. It would have been challenging enough had there been a paved road, or even a gravel road. But there wasn't. No, they had to haul the ungainly burden over rocks and boulders, and over soils well-trodden by the thousands of hippies, seekers, Indians, Hindus, Buddhists, Pentecostals, and tourists who make the Gathering a destination every Fourth of July.

Thoroughly impressed by their ambition, my friend and I expressed marvel at their undertaking. The young man with the long, untrimmed beard and mustache turned to us and stated matter-of-factly, that they were taking the piano to the site in order to call in the Aliens. We both were now doubly impressed. "Cool!" They with their 333-pound burden climbed that ascent with ease, while we flatlanders, carrying only our water bottles and snack bars, struggled to make it to the top.

Several minutes later we noticed a luminous, yellow-green, elongated ellipsoid in the sky. It was moving horizontally from our left at a very slow pace. And when it was directly over the prayer circle at the top of the mountain, it descended vertically until we could no longer see it because of the trees. I turned to my companion and said, "They must've made it to the top!"

Rock art at the astronomical site at Roundy Crossing.

Enter into My Rest

Our Divinity, layer 3

12

COSMIC LOVE OF CHRIST

"I did not come to call the righteous, but sinners."
(Matthew 9:14)

Several months and a thousand miles later, same residence...

In the autumn of the following year two friends and I drove to Virginia Beach on a pilgrimage. It would be my first time visiting the Association for Research and Enlightenment, so I was very excited. Our first layover was just outside Charleston, West Virginia. We camped at beautiful Beech Fork State Park, among the pine trees, beneath the mountains.

Early the next morning I was taken up in spirit. I was shown the Morning Star, brilliant in the clear blue sky. A voice filled the valley, "You are Shiloh." And I was returned to my body.

We resumed our journey to the beach, arriving late that afternoon, and set up camp among the persimmon trees right on Chesapeake Bay. We were exhausted, so we retired early.

The next morning, we went straight to the association headquarters, and without hesitation straight up to the meditation room. I sat down in the row closest to the window in order to enjoy the view of the Atlantic Ocean. It had

Enter into My Rest

been sixteen years since I'd seen it. I closed my eyes to meditate. Immediately I was filled with light: first black, then red, then yellow, then white. Edgar Cayce spoke, "There is someone who wants to meet you!"

Immediately every cell of my being was saturated with the unadulterated Love of God as Jesus and Mary entered.

They remained silent in that space, simply allowing me to experience the totality of their Love. Although they were invisible in that Light, I could feel their Holy Presence. I was speechless. For a few short moments I sat there enjoying the Love of God. And then it was gone.

> "I am the Light of the world; he who follows me
> will not walk in the darkness
> but will have the Light of life."
> (John 8:12)

It is not a metaphor.

Imagine every cell of your body self-aware of God's pure and incomparable Love. Imagine knowing only that Love that you have been invited to enjoy. And now imagine that Light withdrawing and leaving.

"It would have been better if you had not let me taste that beauty."

No human love has ever held a candle to that.

Our Divinity, layer 4

13

PRAYERS OF RAINBOW LIGHT

Four months, 1,000 miles and one residence later...

Once again there I was in my bed, feverish, trembling, and as good as dead. Suddenly, there arose a warm, roaring flood of energy from below. I knew that I would soon be propelled from my body, so I faced east, assumed the correct posture for meditation and stilled my mind.

It's not that I had fear. I didn't. But I've always felt it helps to know where I'm going when I set out on a journey. I'd been out of my body often enough, but this time was different: I would be given volitional control. So, I resolved to set a destination in my mind and to go there.

I controlled my breath, focused my attention on a point behind my eyebrows, and waited. It did not take long. With the force of a rocket blasting off I entered the spirit world. As planned, I went straight up to a place I had seen from afar in meditation: the circle of beings continually sending intercessory prayer to all humanity. It's like a beautiful ring of glorious, white light.

I joined that prayer circle, holding hands with Jesus on my left and another soul on my right. All of us there were humanoid beings of pristine white with a lining of radiant, golden light. From each of our hearts flowed a rainbow directed at the earth.

I was only allowed to be there a brief moment before I was thrust forcibly back into my body. It was a very exhilarating experience!

TRUST YOUR OWN EXPERIENCE

A few months, two miles, and one residence later...

When I was a younger man and you were a toddler, I showed you the wonders of our oneness. I showed you energetic spheres of blue light to entertain you when you awoke afraid in your bed in the middle of the night. Or when you were sad and crying, I showed you the songbirds of light on my shoulders, the motion of their fluttering wings momentarily distracting you enough that you forgot all about your grief and fear.

When you were in an unstable state of mind, overwhelmed by the din of our technological culture, I showed you mental pictures of Kauai: palm trees waving in the breeze, gentle ocean ripples breaking on coral reefs, volcanic mountains against a backdrop of beautiful blue skies, and the bouquet of Plumeria everywhere. You laughed!

When you were a bit older and we were waiting in line to hear the African drum group playing at Nature's Table, I told you about the time I saw multiple rainbows on the horizon when I was a child just about your age. And, as is appropriate for young boys of your age, you blurted out, "I don't believe you!"

So, I asked, "I'll show you. Do you want to see?" You consented. I told you to put your forehead against mine and showed you the picture in my mind's eye. And you saw it! "Okay, okay!" you said, backing away, your rational mind questioning the very thing you had just seen. But you were not afraid, and you allowed me to show you some more pictures. You saw them all!

Another time, when you were in second grade, you fell on the playground, whacking your head on the gravel. You were always one of the tough kids, but I could see your eyes welling up with the tears you fought so hard to hold back. I knelt down beside where you lay and asked if I could help you. Proud and tough, you weren't going to accept the offer. But I affirmed that I really could help, and you relented. With my inner vision I looked inside your head. There where your head had met the gravel hard was a cube of black-red pain. With my spiritual forefinger and thumb I pulled that cube gently out of your head. When it was removed entirely, I handed it to the angels that attend me for that purpose, so that the energy might be recycled, purified and transmuted. You were instantly relieved.

Another time, when you were an adult, we worked together in the kitchen at a nursing home. I had dish washer duty that day. When I was finished, I returned to the kitchen to see what I might do to help you. There you were with your hand wrapped up with ice. "What happened?" I asked. You responded that you'd been carrying a pot of boiling oil, but your hand became weak and the pot began to fall. In the process you poured the oil directly onto your other hand. Fran told you to ice it, but this injury was far worse than mere icing.

I'd never outed myself to you before, but this time I had to expose myself for your sake. "Let me see the burn if I may." You offered the hand. I could see the severity of the damage and I could feel the intensity of the pain. I said, "This is going to hurt." And you consented. I opened myself so that the healing energy of God might come in and remove the burn. It was extremely bad. In the process I felt the boiling oil, and you winced from the re-experience of the pain. It took a few minutes, but the damaged tissue was restored. Only a tiny spot of pink skin remained. "Is that better?" Smiling, you responded, "I always knew you were special."

And then there was the time you and I were on the phone. You were in Virginia and I was in Wisconsin. All of a sudden you had a seizure. I felt helpless to say the least, what with 1,000 miles between us. I began to pray a rosary for you. And, unexpectedly but not surprisingly, Gladys and Gertrude, two of your friends from the other side, appeared to me. They told me to call the administrator of your residence, which I did. Within minutes the ambulance was there to whisk you off to the hospital! You have very good friends, indeed!

Our Divinity, layer 5

PART TWO
GO UP TO THE MOUNTAIN
AND CRY FOR A VISION

Enter into My Rest

Mt Humphreys, one of the most sacred mountains in the American Southwest (photo by the author).

15

SQUIRREL BREAKS AN ARM

Animals can see, hear and feel things that we humans generally cannot.

One thousand miles, one residence and a few months later...

Early in my spiritual journey I studied healing with Harold. One day, while walking to work, I was standing at the intersection of Lincoln Avenue and Oregon Street. It's not much of a thoroughfare compared to big city streets. But in my college town of about 150,000 souls, Lincoln Avenue is one of the major north-south arteries: divided, four lanes, and very busy at rush hour.

The light to the south had just turned green. Suddenly a gray squirrel dashed out into the street directly in front of the oncoming traffic! And from a dozen yards away I heard an audible crack as a black sedan drove over the squirrel's forearm. That poor injured animal ran in huge circles, he was so crazed with pain.

Without thinking, I walked out into the street, not looking to my right or to my left. I shouted to the squirrel, "Come here! I can help you!" Having a better assessment of the situation, the squirrel bounded over to the west side of the avenue. I realized instantly that the squirrel was behaving more rationally than I, for I was now standing right in the way of the oncoming traffic!

Slowly I crossed the avenue, holding my hands before me so that the healing energy could flow to the squirrel waiting for me on the other side. He was looking at me over his left shoulder, clearly cautious, but not budging an inch as I drew closer and closer. The squirrel then did something unexpected. He turned to me and offered up the broken arm.

An intense, tangible flash of bright green light entered into my arm from above and to my right. It flashed into the squirrel. In an instant the arm was healed completely, and the squirrel dashed off like a shot, running on all fours. I was so traumatized by the experience of the squirrel's injury that I couldn't walk by that intersection for months!

At the time, I thought Harold was standing in spirit behind me. Maybe it was an angel. I don't know. What I can say with certainty is it wasn't me. I simply don't know how to do such things. But that squirrel listened to my voice, saw an entity behind me, and knew exactly what to do!

16

POSSUM SAVES TWO LIVES

A few months and two miles later, same residence...

Many thousands of years ago Wisconsin glacial ice covered portions of the Upper Midwest. As the ice melted, long terminal moraines, up to one hundred feet high in places, crossed the landscape like graceful calligraphy. In time, tundra gave way to tall-grass prairie, attracting great herds of bison. Their millions of stomping hooves effectively created the so-called Buffalo Trace, the first major overland highway in this part of the country. The rich glacial soil attracted the Indians to this area. The abundance of game and maize allowed them to sustain a village, while the Buffalo Trace provided them the means to trade with other people to the east and to the northwest.

I used to walk to the edge of town in order to meditate. It was often my only opportunity to escape the psychic din of the city. My first time there I just took a seat on the nearest available mound and sat down to enjoy the anticipated peace and quiet. The mound was relatively low, soft, and without gravel or stones. It seemed perfect.

As I was meditating, however, the faint but ever so distinct aroma of cow manure wafted my way! I looked around to see if I could identify the source of the smell. To the south was a great field of corn with no evidence of bovine fertilizer. To the north were modest middle class houses and apartments. And then I looked down and examined the texture of the "soil" on which I was sitting. It was an old pile of well-cured manure! My hands, clothes and shoes all smelled of poop! My friends derived great pleasure from the tale. "See how much more enlightened you are already!"

Needless to say, I had to find another place to meditate. That I found at the far southern border of that cornfield, near a lone tree that embodied special power. It would be some time later that I learned that only a few yards from that tree was a vortex that functioned as a natural doorway to the spirit world.

When I went there to meditate the spirits of the ancestors would appear to me. Only the women and children showed me their joyous faces, inviting me to come join the great picnic in the spirit world. The chiefs and warriors showed me their backs, because I hadn't earned their respect by performing acts of valor.

One time while I was seated there I saw a possum lying dead in the flooded culvert to my right. I asked the spirits, "What is the best way to deal with the corpse in a respectful way?" The chiefs behind me replied with some disdain, "Where do the people bury their dead?" Recognizing that burial grounds were often atop a hill so that winds could purify the remains and clear the air, I pulled the possum out of the culvert. Immediately her twin possum babies fled from the marsupial's pouch and ran into the pipe through which the water flowed. Their lives had been saved. Their mother had been honored.

Many other events occurred at my meditation spot, including visions of "the Watchers," who are fifty- or sixty-foot-tall spiritual beings that appear simply to watch. And I had visions of seven eagles flying west, each a different radiant color of the rainbow, as well as a vision of the pink-hued vortex, in which I used to sit to meditate.

Years later I learned that this was the site of the largest ancient village in the area. The state archaeological society had protected the village with very effective camouflage. They farmed it!

RATTLESNAKE PICKS A FIGHT

wo years, 2,000 miles, and one residence later, but now homeless again...

Events told me to "Give the wheel of fortune a spin." So I did. There was no debt, there were no dependents, there was no property, and there were no assets. So I gathered all my possessions consisting of a Bible, a change of clothes, a copy of *The Nag Hammadi Library*, note cards with bibliographic information from my research, my toiletries, and what little cash I had, and I went up to the mountain. A friend dropped me off at the trailhead to the Siskiyou National Forest, and I set my sites on Bald Mountain in the Kalmiopsis Wilderness. Another friend, Lou, was the self-appointed advocate for the wilderness. My intention was to stay with him at his primitive camp while I awaited my vision.

There are actually several distinct forests there: white pines or oaks on the flats along the Illinois River, young aspens colonizing the burns left by ancient forest fires, and at the peaks 700- or more year-old stands of ancient Douglas firs. All of these were sparsely peppered with scrawny madrones vainly reaching up to the sunlight beneath the overspreading canopy, and the ubiquitous Manzanita bushes colonized the serpentine soils wherever they could get a foothold. There were a few poison oaks to boot. Huckleberry bushes, bear grass, and Oregon grape covered the forest floor.

I met Lou at the peak on the ridgeline path as ancient as the mountain, where the Takelma had hunted and perhaps summered. He'd shown up like the answer to prayer. I'd intuitively found his old camp, but the only water supply had dried up, and he'd moved to a new camp just a hundred yards away. When we were catching up on old acquaintances, and I had shared the dreams that had brought me to this place in life, I happened to mention that I'd stashed some items at the trailhead. He chastised me forcefully, and ordered me to return to the bottom of the mountain to retrieve those possessions. Leaving anything on the forest is strictly prohibited!

The next morning I started early, as it is a dozen miles and 3,000 feet down. It became an adventure in its own right, what with encounters with a bear and a great herd of deer. I'd packed a tent, a sleeping bag, and some snack bars.

The path in the ancient forest at the top is a mere nine to twelve inches wide. To my left the slope plunged more or less straight down to Silver Creek hundreds of feet below. To my right were sheer, damp, mossy outcrops of bedrock. Here everything is in shadow all day every day. The force of the mountain seemed to repel me, as two magnets of the same charge repel each other, such that it felt as if an unseen arm were trying to push me off.

Leaving the 10,000-year-old forest untouched by glaciers and therefore one of the most botanically diverse places on earth, bushwhacking down the washed out path, through the aspen forest, and through the bleached white bones of a fire long past, I finally reached the Illinois River Canyon.

Enter into My Rest

And there it was, only inches away, directly in front of me, a rattlesnake coiled and rattling. It was relatively young, only four rattles and about eighteen inches long. And given the canyon terrain, there was no option for me. I would have to use the path. Uphill would require a steep climb up the slippery, serpentine slope, and downhill a slide all the way to the river below.

Harold had told me that humanity had been given authority over all the animals. So I, having no fear whatsoever, addressed the snake, "I know you are sunning yourself. I don't intend you any harm. I just need to walk on this path to get down the mountain. If you go off the path, I'll pass by and you can come right back to continue sunning yourself." The rattlesnake uncoiled, slithered off the path, and I continued my descent down the mountain.

18

BIGFOOT ON THE MOUNTAIN

Three weeks and twenty-four miles later, and still homeless...

It gets very cold atop the mountain. Though we were camped only 4,000 feet up, when the brisk Pacific winds blow 100 mph or more, the air temperature drops below freezing, even in the middle of the summer. I had only a few changes of clothes, a cream-colored, faux leather aviator-style jacket, and a sleeping bag to warm myself when I slept.

That night I knew it would be a long night of shivering and withdrawing deeply into myself. Even the voles, who'd regularly burrowed up to the surface beneath my nylon pup tent to steal my heat through the sheer floor, even they had sufficient sense to go deep underground that particular night.

Then out of the dark night two very large beings lay down by my tent, one on either side of it. They were each longer than my tent, perhaps as much as eight feet from head to toe. They were emitting so much radiant energy I could see it. And with their generous gift of themselves, I slept as soundly as a child in its mother's arms.

Harold and his family had experienced their presence. One time their youngest, then only two years of age and not in control of her gifts, teleported herself alone to an area of the forest without her parents' knowledge. It took them hours to find her. When they did they found her playing with a Bigfoot family. They'd been babysitting until her parents arrived!

These certainly weren't black bears that night, though several lived nearby. Being the largest four-legged mammals in the area, they made no effort to conceal their presence. Unlike the cougar whose silence is legendary, the bears literally crashed through the huckleberry bushes rather than going around! These particular bears were not afraid of us, one or more of them having reached into the tent of some local kids who'd joined us for a weekend. The bears had smelled the kids' snack bars, unzipped the tent, and grabbed the bars while the kids slept!

One time I was given the job of keeping the fire while the others went up to pray at the ceremonial circle on the peak. Two bears walked through the camp no more than ten yards from me. Periodically the bears would raid the latrine in search of some fast food! No, my ad hoc infrared-light sources were not a pair of black bears gratuitously bringing me comfort!

And there is only one other being I know that could be that tall and that quiet. Bigfoot!

19

CALLED OUT OF CHALDEA

Four-hundred and fifty miles, two residences and nine months later...

When I came down off the mountain, I spent nine months in Portland, Oregon. I'd been planning on moving to the commune upriver from the canyon near the California border. They needed an English teacher and I needed a job. Temporary accommodations in the form of a 1,000-square-foot, two-story yurt would have been provided.

The commune was in the middle of the old-growth forest in a valley beneath the towering Siskiyou Mountains, just northeast of the Redwood Forest. I was really looking forward to leaving the city and going to the sunshine of southern Oregon. The healthier environment and lifestyle appealed to me tremendously. But everything changed in the blink of an eye. The yurt was no longer available.

A few weeks earlier I had visited a friend who lived in Queen Anne, Seattle. He and his wife had a houseful of beautiful little girls, and they were in great need of a nanny. They'd invited me to come and stay with them any time. And I still needed a job. So, holding them to their word, I took the train from Portland to Seattle and surprised them!

Enter into My Rest

Unknown to me, my friends were receiving guests who had just returned stateside from China, where they'd been teaching English as a second language. They already had tickets for the connecting flight from Seattle to Chicago, but after two flights and several days in transit, they couldn't stomach boarding one more jet. So they were staying a couple days with my friends, trying to figure out how to find another way home.

The next day I felt obliged to write to my dad to let him know I was now in Seattle. But as I was writing the letter, a divine lightning bolt struck my heart. Without a word being spoken, I understood that I had to return to the Midwest. It was the last place I ever wanted to be, but I knew it would be the best thing for all parties involved.

My friends needed to sell their car. Their friends had the money, but being dead tired from their flights, they needed a third driver. I needed a ride to Chicago. Voilá! Within 36 hours, I was back in my hometown. Several years later, Jesus would tell me that I had great faith for obeying that call.

20

PLEIADEAN QUANTUM PHYSICS

Three thousand miles, six years and six residences later...

After six years of service to humanity for the love of God I moved to Virginia Beach in order to study at a small private college. It was a trial. I was lucky to have one meal a day. The work available was menial and the pay scale was quite low.

That fall I suffered from sciatica so badly that I was in pain whether standing, sitting, or lying down. One night I was taken up in spirit and introduced to the Pleiadians. They were shorter than the average adult human being, with a distinct yellow-green hue, large eyes, and enlarged crania. We Sufi danced together!

The next night I was taken up in spirit and I was with them again. I looked at the Pleiadian directly in front of me and pleaded, "Can you heal my sciatica?" Even now I can feel the anguish as I implored him to help me. What happened next was unexpected. That Pleiadian uploaded quantum equations of yellow light into my body. There was a tremendous volume of data resembling graphs, equations, and subatomic particle trajectories. It was information. And in the process, the sciatica was healed! It took me more than twenty years to learn the physics principles encoded in that upload.

Enter into My Rest

Our Divinity, layer 6

2 1

SPIRITUAL WARRIOR

One thousand miles, three residences and two or three years later...

In my mid-thirties I began to explore my Indian roots with great passion. I pursued every cultural and spiritual opportunity that presented itself, from pipe ceremonies and sweat lodges to archaeological excavations and seasonal powwows.

At one of my first powwows, a young dancer caught my eye. He was quite young, not even twenty years old, with high cheek bones, ebony hair, and brown eyes. He'd only just begun competing, so his regalia consisted of a bustle, a roach, a loin cloth of sorts, a feather fan, and a sky-blue kerchief. His spirit was noble, proud, and radiant.

That particular weekend, I went to the powwow four times. It resonated in my heart. And I loved to watch the dance competitions. While observing and later participating in the Hopi Serpent Dance, a voice spoke to me. "He has a gift he wants to give you." And my heart was filled with the same love I'd experienced when I'd met Jesus and Mary in spirit twelve years earlier. I didn't know what the gift was.

I went over to the dance arena to watch the competitions. Once again my heart was filled with that Divine Love. And the emcee stated, "If you are inspired to do something at the powwow, it is our belief that you should do it. Don't leave with regrets."

Nevertheless, I went home that night. When I awoke the next morning I learned that I'd developed a cough, ostensibly because of exposure. In my heart, I knew it was actually due to the words left unspoken. The emcee's words haunted me. And I did have regret. Originally I had planned to stay home that Sunday, but now I knew I had to go back to the powwow.

I wanted to give that young man a gift, but the only thing I had to share was a small Egyptian cobra pendant on a leather thong. She, Buto, was the patron deity of Northern Egypt, the eye of Ra and the protector of Pharaoh. So I put on my best powwow clothes, wrapped up Buto in red cloth, and returned to the powwow for the fourth time in three days.

At the powwow I stood on the west side of the arena, just to the right of the emcee. It was a long wait. Finally the young dancer came into the arena with an entourage of women. I waited for the right moment to approach him. Eventually an opportunity presented itself, and I asked if I might speak with him. He said, "Yes".

I asked him his tribe. "Menominee." I asked if there were some way I might support him. I wanted to give him money. Noble, honorable, embracing the values of his culture, he replied, "If you would support me, support the people," as he swept his arm around the arena. "And dance the intertribals." He spoke to me in the traditional high-pitched voice adopted by males of certain tribes to show respect.

I told him I wanted to give him a gift and presented the cobra. Upon seeing it he asked, "Are you sure?"

I responded, "Yes." With that he gave me a piece of his regalia that had great meaning to him. I was more than a little stunned and greatly honored, indeed.

Our Divinity, layer 7

Our Divinity, layer 8

22

DISAPPEARING SWEAT LODGE

Inside every cube is a regular octahedron. Every regular octahedron has six vertices and one center. These are the seven directions...

Twenty miles, a few months later and the same residence...

My first experience in the sweat lodge was particularly intense. I'd prepared myself with focus and sincerity. I'd no idea what to expect, but my prayers and resolve prepared me to receive the spirit of healing when it descended.

The sweat lodge was a more or less permanent structure behind Medicine Bear's doctor's house. It was in an exclusive neighborhood, so privacy was assured. But for me, all of us there were women. Even before the fire was lit I entered into a deep trance-like state.

Once the rocks were white hot, it was time for us to enter the lodge. That night we would be sweating four rounds. And so it began. But something amazing happened: the top of the sweat lodge vanished! It had dissolved into the tangible blackness of infinite inner space. There were objects in my field of view, but my focus was on the Grandmother who appeared just above the now invisible sweat lodge "ceiling." She was looking down upon our hodgepodge gathering, as if to satisfy her curiosity about who we were to have opened that sacred space. Of course, there were two of us with Indian blood, and several who'd been on *bona fide* native paths for some time. The remainder consisted of sincere seekers.

The Grandmother's face was brown and deeply etched, the telltale signs of decades of outdoor living and hard work. There were no exchanged thoughts or words. Only the healing energy.

Another time, at my Anishinaabe friend's house near the headwaters of the Mississippi River, we convened on a beautiful Minnesota night of exceptional clarity. On that particular occasion there were no bells or eagle bone whistles, only the sacred ritual and the purifying heat. But during one of the rounds I was shown that the sweat lodge is the analog of the Holy of Holies in the Jerusalem Temple.

In Jewish mysticism, the Holy of Holies is the Garden of Eden from which Adam and Eve were exiled. It is also the World to Come, to which the worthy will return. It is the Presence of God, where the Throne is. And that is where the angels visit us. All that is called miraculous and righteous belongs therein. There we stand in the Glory of God.

Our Divinity, layer 9

23

CALLING THE EAGLES

The People believe that eagles carry our prayers up to the Creator...

One thousand, six hundred miles, a few months and one residence later...

The very first time I went to visit my folks in Flagstaff, my dad, my sister, and I went to Upper Lake Mary to watch the bald eagles. I had some tobacco in order to offer up prayers to the Creator.

We drove around to the west side of the lake. I walked out onto the lakebed, now bone dry from extended drought. And I sat down. Taking out the tobacco, I thanked the ancestors, Mother Earth, and the Great White Spirit that animates all things. Closing my eyes, I sat there enjoying the peace.

My sister, in her inimitable style, blurted out, "You called the eagles!" There, circling directly overhead, were a half dozen adult bald eagles. Though it had only just begun, my trip was now complete. Ever since it has thrilled me to see the most majestic of all birds soaring, performing their mating rituals, cooing and cawing, fishing, nesting, or just perching on a branch.

Once, many years before that, when I was following a Hindu path, I wanted to offer a butter sacrifice. Metaphorically speaking, clarified butter is the purified heart of the devotee; and offering it in the fire is dedicating it to God.

So, I bought a pound of butter and clarified it in a heavy skillet, skimming off all the dross and milk solids as the butter slowly melted. The fragrance was sensually appealing. I prayed over the butter all the while.

Then I collected small dry sticks, twigs, and pieces of bark. As I intended to make the offering in a small hibachi, I had to scale down the logs for the fire.

So, the time came to offer the sacrifice. I chose an area of the deck away from the house, assembled the sticks, twigs, and bark in the hibachi and ignited it. All the while I was praying. Once the twigs were burning I poured the clarified butter into the fire, one spoonful at a time. The flames leaped up as the butter blazed, carrying the prayers up to the Creator.

Immediately, the space-time continuum was changed. The air became dense as time stood still. And then something completely unexpected happened. The birds came to witness the offering. Two sparrows sat on the deck only a few feet to my left, while two doves and a male cardinal perched on a wire overhead.

Praying, I offered the butter until it was all gone. And the birds remained steadfastly observing, not even ruffling a feather. When the sacrifice had ended, and the fire had burned out, the sacred space closed, and the birds flew away.

Enter into My Rest

24

FROG COMES TO SWEAT

One hundred and fifty miles, one residence and one to two years later...
Red Elk and Snake were hosting a Morning Star sweat event, consisting of five sweats spread out over a four day period. Each would include four rounds of prayer followed by a "Love Feast." Except for the fifth and final one, sweats were held at night. The days were ours to enjoy however we would. After the second nightly sweat, two of the women participants went out drinking at a local bar. The next day all of us in the lodge bore those two participants' hangovers! We had all become one in the process. That's called entanglement... It was a difficult and unpleasant lesson to learn.

A couple of nights, local Indian women joined us. One woman was celebrating the birth of her first child. As this was a traditional sweat, the women wore dresses that covered their bodies from their necks to their ankles, with sleeves all the way down to their wrists. Over this, they wore long sleeved sweaters! They were very quiet and private, choosing not to associate with the rest of us between rounds.

The most interesting event, however, was the fifth and final sweat. That was the time Frog joined us. Each round, after all the human participants had entered the lodge, Frog came in the door and sat behind the sweat lodge leader. He sat there while the prayers were made. And when the round was finished, the humans would exit and Frog followed! A bit of a loner, Frog sat just outside the door awaiting the next round! This particular sweat included a fifth round for the Morning Star. And, as with the previous four rounds, Frog waited until all the humans had entered, and then followed us in. And, after all had departed the lodge for the last time, Frog came out and hopped away!

What boggled our minds was that with an internal temperature well over 200° F above the rock pit at the center of the sweat lodge, that little, soft-skinned creature managed not to get cooked!

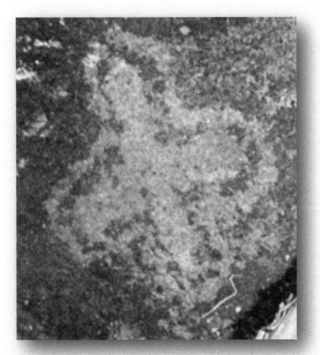

A petroglyph of Morning Star at the astronomical site, Roundy Crossing.

Enter into My Rest

25

SPIRITS IN THE SWEAT LODGE

Six hundred miles, months later, and the same residence...

Contrary to the beliefs of some of my friends, drugs are not used in the traditional sweat lodge ceremony. The experience of the two partying women at the Morning Star sweat was evidence enough. But there was another event that reinforced the teaching. Red Elk had told me that alcohol must be avoided at least three days prior to participating in the ceremony.

One summer evening, seven of us convened at Snake's house near the headwaters of the Mississippi River. Red Elk took me aside and told me that one of the participants had a problem with alcohol and psychological abuse. Ostensibly he, his wife and his daughter were there for group therapy. Red Elk told me that he and Brother Bob would not be going in, and he asked me if I would be going in under the circumstances. I told him, "I'll go in, but I'll sit at the door opposite Snake," thereby placing me as far from the family as possible.

The first round proceeded normally. Nothing unusual happened. But the second round was quite different. I heard someone blowing an eagle bone whistle. I thought it was Red Elk. The whistle played off and on throughout the round. When I opened my eyes, I saw rosy-lavender plasma rising up serpent-like out of the rock pit. It wasn't steam. It wasn't the brilliant orange or white-hot sparkling rocks. The wisps of plasma occurred several times, always rising up and out of the top of the lodge. This happened again during the third round, as also did the playing of the eagle bone whistle. The fourth round, like the first, was normal.

Afterward, I was walking down the long drive that led up to the property, just enjoying the fresh Northwoods air, looking at the starry sky, and being alone with my thoughts. After a while Red Elk came over to me and asked me if I'd heard the eagle bone whistle. "Yes," I said. "I thought it was you."

"No. The whistling was coming out of the fire pit!"

"Wow!" I was genuinely stunned. I shared, "In the sweat lodge during the second and third rounds, rosy-lavender wisps of plasma-like light came up out of the rocks. It happened several times. It was like *Indiana Jones and the Raiders of the Lost Ark!*"

Red Elk told me that alcoholics bring along spirits with them. Perhaps the wisps of plasma were the spirits departing their host. I don't know, but I was and continue to be very thankful for my guardian angels that protect me from such things!

26

THINGS THAT GO BUMP IN THE LIGHT

Twelve thousand miles, three residences and five to six years later...

I'd like to say that the archangel Gabriel appears to me, hands me a tape measure, and says, "Measure the Temple." But no, the reality for me is quite different. I usually experience the physical push of some invisible spirit impelling my body in one direction or another.

Over the years, I've participated in numerous archaeological expeditions. Once in New Mexico, while surveying Bureau of Land Management land in preparation for a road-building project, one or more of the ancestors came to me and actually moved my body to show me a rather nondescript pile of rocks in the otherwise sandy terrain. Right before my eyes, that rock pile transformed into a structure. It was as if I were seeing through someone else's eyes.

In my usual survey style, I began to circle the pile in an ever-diminishing spiral, all the while looking for anything that didn't belong. And it didn't take long for me to find the first artifact: a flake of obsidian, the remains of a nodule transported from a volcano some fifty miles away. Eventually our team found, documented, and collected several dozen artifacts surrounding what many centuries earlier had been a hunting blind.

Remains of a hunting blind near El Rito, New Mexico.

Another time, on a survey in Arizona, I noted a depression beyond what appeared to be a bower, an entrance to an apparent glade surrounded by scraggy junipers. The soil in the depression was tinged pale carmine-rose. It was sandier and less dense than the surrounding pale umber organic soils. I walked into the center of the depression. Immediately, some unseen force impelled me backward, away from the center toward the bower "door." I was being told to look. I spoke to the ancestors and asked, "What do you want me to see?"

My survey partner was a spry grandmother who volunteered, "There is nothing here. Just some burnt wood from a forest fire."

I knew otherwise.

Enter into My Rest

The remains of the Hohokam pit house.

I walked away in search of the project leader, Heather. When I found her, I asked, "Would you come with me? I don't know what I am seeing."

With the sweet graciousness of a soul made whole with self-respect and patience, Heather followed me to the glade. Within minutes, our group had successfully identified the remains of a Hohokam semi-subterranean pit house. The surface was still littered with shards of paddle-and-anvil redware that the Hohokam traded with the neighboring cultures. We found the shards where they had dropped perhaps 1,200 years previously. The discovery of the heretofore unknown outpost demonstrated the presence of the Hohokams in that area several centuries before the pueblo builders whose houses we were documenting.

An example of Hohokam paddle-and-anvil redware.

Then there was the time I was 'told' to measure a city. At first I didn't get the message, but later I was shown the brilliance of the culture that built it. This happened at Cahokia.

Though I'd been there a dozen times, I'd never taken pictures of anything but the equinoctial sunrise over Monks Mound. This time I went with the sole intention of photographing everything. And I intended to record in a notebook the identity of each mound photographed, so that I wouldn't have to depend on my memory.

Enter into My Rest

Equinoctial sunrise photographed from west of the center of the Woodhenge at Cahokia.

I arrived in Collinsville, Illinois late in the afternoon. As there were several hours' daylight remaining, I drove out to the site and began with the mounds closest to the parking lot. At first, everything went well.

When I crossed over into the Underworld half of the site, after having taken several photographs and documenting them, my only pen disappeared. I searched my pockets, I searched my shirt. I searched my socks, my fanny pack, backpack, jacket, T-shirt collar, even inside my T-shirt. I searched inside my cap! There was no pen to be found. I paced up and down the only

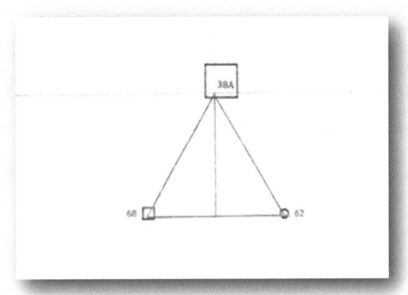

A map of the primary equilateral triangle at Cahokia.

Monks Mound, Cahokia, from the south.

Enter into My Rest

path I'd trodden, thinking I might have dropped my pen along the way, but to no avail. There was no pen on the ground. Though I'd intended to continue until dusk, it was now impossible. So I packed my gear and headed back on the path to my car.

As soon as I left the Underworld half of the site and crossed into the Upper World half, my pen reappeared! It was exactly where it was supposed to have been, in the very place I'd searched at least three times! I recognized the involvement of the ancestors, but only much later would I learn why. They were preparing to reveal the sacred geometry of the site.

27

CREATION, COSMOS, AND CAHOKIA

hirteen years, 60,000 miles and six residences later...

I was taken up in Spirit. All was tangible black light, just as it was before the dawn. I was given a seat among the Council of Elders. The chief engineer, one of the grandmothers, was explaining the design of the future city. She had before her a holographic model of Cahokia.

Pointing to the emerald-green, hexagonal crystal of light, she spoke, "This is the channel of energy coming from the Upper World and flowing into this world. It represents the link between the celestial Orion and its terrestrial analog. Its cross-section will be a regular hexagon comprised of six equilateral triangles all sharing one common point that marks the Tree of Life. Each side of the six triangles will measure 969 units. Each apex of each triangle will be marked by a pyramidal or conical structure. The people in Colombia will preserve this knowledge, which will also be encoded in the design of Cahokia.

Then, pointing to the primary equilateral triangle, she spoke, "These are the hearth stones. This information will be kept by the people of Ichkabal, as well as encoded in the design of the city. The hearthstones are also a part of Orion. These are at the base of the Tree of Life.

Enter into My Rest

Then she pointed to a holographic diamond of light, whose vertices pointed to the cardinal directions. Again she spoke, "This diamond embodies the knowledge that will be preserved by our cousins who travelled east when our people travelled west. Each of the four terrestrial vertices will be marked by its own sacred lodge consisting of upright posts in a circle. Another lodge will be

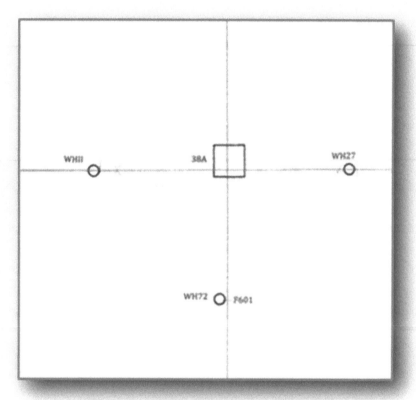

The map of the Woodhenges and the location
of the Tree of Life at the center.

Looking due east from the center of Woodhenge with Monks Mound in the distance.

constructed beneath the place where the Tree of Life will stand. After a dedication ceremony the lodge beneath the tree will be covered over by the metaphorical mountain. The Tree of Life will emerge from this mountain."

I saw the image of a celestial ceremonial lodge directly above the Tree of Life.

And again she spoke, "The east and west terrestrial vertices of the diamond crystal will coincide with two of the mounds marking the equilateral triangles. Thus each diagonal of the octahedral diamond will measure twice 969 units."

Then I was taken to the south side of a great pyramid of light. The grandmother handed me a length of rope and commanded, "Measure the pyramid." The first terrace on which the Tree of Life would be erected measured 95 units west of the stairway and 57 units east of the stairway leading up to the third and fourth terraces.

She asked me, "Do you know what these mean?"

Monks Mound from the southeast, showing Terrace 1.

"No, but you know. Tell me."

"These are the hypotenuse and base of a 3-4-5 right triangle. It is one of the building blocks of the Universe. The first terrace must be built like a layer cake with alternating soft and rigid layers, in order that it will withstand geological disturbances. This terrace must survive. It is a measuring device meant to preserve the knowledge, lest the people forget."

Monks Mound from the east showing Terraces 1, 3 and 4.

Enter into My Rest

28

SACRED GEOMETRY

Then I was taken aloft over the greatest truncated pyramid. There was intentional "damage" designed into the fabric of the second terrace. It resembled a great crack in the carapace of a giant turtle. A Tree of Life was growing out of this crack and going up to the sky.

And Grandmother told me that each of the highest terraces measured 57 units along the north-south axis. She asked, "Do you know what this means?"

"No."

"This length equals the world's polar circumference divided by 2,700 sacred 260 day counts."

"Why is that?" I asked.

And she answered, "Time and space are one. The cosmos was carefully made in order that humanity might remember how she fits into the fabric of Creation, into the web of life. Without the knowledge, how can humanity possibly create anything? This is the Cosmic Sweat Lodge.

"These are the tools of creation: the 3-4-5 right triangle, the octahedron, the equilateral triangle and the unity of time and space. Remember this…"

PART THREE
IN THE SPIRIT WORLD

Our Divinity, layer 10

29

VISION OF THE JERUSALEM TEMPLE

Revelation 11:15-19

Imagine you have just arrived in Jerusalem for a tour of the Temple. Only ritually pure people can ascend to the Temple Mount, and in the minds of the members of the Qumran Community, where the Dead Sea Scrolls were copied, **only ritually pure people can even enter the city**! So, having immersed yourself in the mikvah, and having become both morally and ritually pure, you begin your ascent to the Temple Mount. It's several hundred feet up Mount Moriah if you're coming from the Lower City, and considerably more if you're coming from one of the surrounding valleys!

When you get to the ridgeline of Mount Moriah you have to ascend one of the stairways just to get to the gates of the Temple Mount, the artificially leveled platform surrounding the Temple. Back in Solomon's day the Temple Mount was 500 cubits north to south, and 500 cubits east to west. Access was only through a few gates by which you could enter the "Court of the Gentiles." Only those who have denied the evil inclinations of their heart may enter here.

Enter into My Rest

A low balustrade, called the soreg, separates the Court of the Gentiles from the rest of the complex. Our guides lead us to the east side of the courtyard, near the Susa Gate and Solomon's Portico. Here it is that Jesus walked: "It was winter, when Hanukkah occurs in Jerusalem. Jesus was walking in the temple precinct, in Solomon's Portico.

The Judeans surrounded him and said, 'How long will you keep us in suspense? If you are the Messiah, tell us frankly.'" (John 10:22-24)

The Golden Gate on the East Side of the Temple Mount
(Photograph courtesy of Pastor Eric Meyer, MDiv.)

Another time, after healing the lame man, Peter and John were walking through Solomon's Portico when the amazed crowds ran after them. (Acts 3:11)

And not long thereafter,

"By the hands of the Apostles many signs and wonders happened among the people. And all were of one mind in Solomon's Portico." (Acts 5:12)

Imagine we are privy to one of these sermons, as we contemplate the Mount of Olives across the Kidron Valley to the east. This is a place of inspiration, education and miracles.

The next stop on the tour brings us into the "Women's Court." It is a perfect square, 135 cubits on each side. In Jesus' day the Israelite women assembled here. These were the mothers and wives, the grandmothers and daughters, the compassionate and loving ones, the pillars of the family, the nurturers and the counselors to their husbands, fathers and sons. Servant girls and women prophets alike intermingled here.

It is not by accident that the collection boxes are in this courtyard, as the women are the "economists" of the household and managed the resources. It is the mothers whose genealogies determined the eligibility of the men to be ethnic Israelites. Well over 4000 standing people fit comfortably in this area, where voices are raised in songs of joy. We, too, can join in with devotional songs, all with one voice, raising the roof with the harmonies and ever so subtle overtones, rising and falling, ebbing and fading, lifting up our spirits and intoxicating our senses, a beloved hymn to the Most High. This is a place of reverence.

Ascending yet more stairs, we enter into the Inner Court that surrounds the House of God. Though this court is one continuous unit, the space is divided

Enter into My Rest

quite unequally into several areas. The foremost part of the court is the Israelites' Court. Though it is the most sanctified place non-Levitical Israelites could enter, it is rather small. It measures only eleven cubits by 135 cubits. Only a few hundred fit comfortably within this area.

View of the Mount of Olives from the vicinity of the Dome of the Tablets. (Photo courtesy Pastor Eric Meyer, MDiv.)

Beyond this is the altar, elevated high above the adjacent courtyard. The ramp leading up to it, on which the priests carry up the offerings, is 30 cubits in length! Portions of the offerings were used to sustain the priests and their families, and the community's widows and orphans. Though we no longer make offerings in this way, we can offer up sacrifices on the altar of our hearts. Here let us offer up envy, bitterness, hatred, anger, fantasies and the guilt they engender. Let us offer up all the hurt we've suffered at the hands of our abusers. Let us offer up hopelessness, apathy and resentment. And let us continue to offer up everything until all that remains are the gifts that were guaranteed the moment we received the Spirit.

The fruits of the spirit are selfless love, joy, peace, long-suffering,
mercy, charity, faith, humility and self-control.
(Galatians 5:22-23)

You might notice you are beginning to glow! This is a place of transformation.

Looking around the courtyard we notice several furnishings. Once, over there, were the ten lavers that Solomon commissioned. These consisted of ten basins, each supported by a quadrangular brazen base. On the sides of the basins were carved the images of a lion, an eagle and a bull. The same were carved on the supporting pillars that were situated at the corners. All the bases stood atop four wheels, such that...

Anyone who saw the spokes of the wheels, how exactly they were turned,
and united to the sides of the bases, and with what harmony
they agreed to the felloes, would wonder at them.
(Josephus, Antiquities 8.81-83)

Enter into My Rest

This description brings to mind the vision of the Chariot:

> *...as to the form of their faces, the face of a man...the face of a lion...the face of a bull...and the face of an eagle...as I looked at the living beings, behold, there was one wheel on the earth...for the four of them. The appearance of the wheels like...beryl, their appearance and workmanship as the wheel in the midst of the wheel.*
> *(Ezekiel 1:10, 15-16)*

The images of the cherubim remind us we are approaching the Throne of Glory where there are troops of cherubim and flaming seraphim.

Across the court is the porch of the Sanctuary. In Jesus' day there were no doors on the porch,

> *For it represented the universal visibility of heaven...*
> *(Josephus, Wars of the Jews 5:208).*

Let us climb the last set of stairs and respectfully walk into the place only the priests could enter and then only one priest at a time. The walls are decorated with palm trees, gourds, open flowers and cherubim, symbolizing the Garden of Eden and the cherubim posted at its borders.

In the Second Temple a veil embroidered in blue, linen, scarlet and purple covered the doorway leading into the Sanctuary. On the veil was embroidered all that was mystical in the heavens, except the zodiac signs. We know that in ancient cosmology the constellations of the night sky were located beyond the seventh heaven and represented the boundary between the material world and the heavenly realms. Once we cross this threshold, we are leaving the mundane and familiar and entering into the cosmic realms. Emphasizing this cosmic threshold are the seven lamps representing the seven (then) known planets and the twelve loaves of showbread representing the zodiac and the year. This place is cosmic in scope and here, in the last few steps before entering the Holy of Holies, we have been lifted up into supernatural realms. How can we not be in awe?

At the end of this room is the altar of incense, where the 24 priestly families are allowed to serve 91 days spread out over a six-year period, one priest at a time, to offer up incense and prayer to the Most High. This, in fact, is the very room in which Gabriel announced to Zachariah the birth of John the Baptist! John tells us that the smoke of the incense offered on this alter represents the prayers of the righteous. (Revelation 8:3-4) Here our daily prayers approach the Throne of Glory just beyond the gold-plated doors leading into the Holy of Holies.

And finally, we have arrived at the threshold. The doors open up to the gold-plated 400-square-cubit room, corresponding to the tenth heaven to which Enoch was summoned by the Lord, who said,

"Have courage, Enoch, fear not, stand before my face into eternity."
(2 Enoch 22)

Before us is the place where the Mercy Seat would have been, still guarded by the carved cherubim that represent the living creatures that surround the throne day and night singing,

"Holy, holy, holy", having four faces: a lion's, an ox's, a human's and an eagle's. (Revelation 4:7-8)

Here, at last we have left the affairs of the world and we, too, are invited to stand before the face of God for all eternity. Here the pervasive white light of his Glory permeates every cell of our beings with unconditional love. Here our hearts are united with his, the very substance of God throbbing our unity of purpose in him. And suddenly...

The angel showed me that the east-west axis of the Jerusalem Temple equaled the radius of the world divided by 42,000. And then the angel showed me that the Temple's east-west axis equaled the polar circumference of the world divided by 264,000. And I marveled at these wonderful measures.

"Do you know what that means?"

I responded, "I have no idea. What does it mean?"

"The length of the Temple equals one Divine Year."

I asked, "How can that be?"

"The Cosmos was designed to teach people the way home. Moses and David received the dimensions that were in exact proportion to the world."

Six more angels descended from above. Each was holding the side of a cube. They spoke with one voice, saying, "This is the Garden of Eden." Embossed on the cube were the Cherubim whose job it is to protect the Garden.

The cube fit inside the Holy of Holies in which the tablets of the covenant were stacked one atop the other in the Ark. Each tablet was six handbreadths long, six handbreadths wide and three handbreadths thick. When stacked they formed a perfect cube.

Outside I saw the Israelites assembled in one place together offering the four species to the six directions. It is the time of the ingathering.

And Enoch asked, "Who of all men is able to understand the breadth and the length of the earth?" And Sirach asked, "...the days of eternity who can enumerate...the breadth of the earth...who can decrypt?" And the angel said, "God can."

Then he took me to the entrance of the House where there stood two columns. One of them had a circumference of twelve cubits. And he asked me, "Do you know what this means?"

Again, I replied, "I have no idea."

"The royal cubit is the sacred ratio 22/42, five of which represent the manifest creative power of God in the world." Then he took me to the Holy of Holies, and he showed me the cherubim that stand over the Mercy Seat. Their wings were five cubits each for both wings, and the height of each cherub was twice five cubits. Then he showed me the Brazen Sea in the House. It had a radius of five cubits, and a depth of five cubits, and a circumference of 30 cubits.

"Sir, isn't that wrong?"

And he replied, "Is it?"

Then he showed me a golden cubit, different in length from the first one.

"What is that?" I asked.

He replied, "The sacred measure used to build the Temple. Six of these cubits equal five of the other."

Then he disappeared.

Enter into My Rest

30

PELICAN DREAM

**"There will be two men in the field; one will be taken
and one will be left. (Matthew 24:40)**

Revelation 11:15-19

"I think it's my dream."

"It is."

It was August 2003. Ira and I are both avid amateur astronomers. Every now and then we'd pull out my dad's old Edmunds Scientific refracting telescope. "This will be the closest that Mars has come to our planet in nearly 60,000 years," said the news release. This would occur on August 27th, only days away.

I was standing in the middle of the Plain City Park. I was looking south toward the row of houses adjacent to and across the street from the park. It was twilight. My attention was drawn to the east as a red planet the size of the moon arose. Then my attention was drawn to the western horizon where I saw the setting sun, the narrowest crescent of the new moon, Venus as the Evening Star, and Jupiter. I saw each of these celestial bodies in exquisite detail.

Once again, my attention was drawn to the red planet. As I watched, a pure white light shining out of the north projected an image of the Western Hemisphere on it. The lakes and mountains, rivers, and plains were clearly visible. Instantly this image was transformed into a seated woman, supporting herself on her right arm and embracing a white pelican with her left arm. The elaborately coifed and classically dressed woman was smiling enigmatically.

A very large crowd had gathered in the park. Jesus was leading them. All those following him were walking from west to east. Jesus began to ascend toward a luminous cross radiating brilliant light. Sathya Sai Baba was bringing up the rear. He turned toward me and beckoned me with a hand gesture to come and join them.

I'd painted a picture of this dream in the summer of 1983. A friend asked, "Shouldn't that be a dove?"

"I thought so, too, until I looked up the Medieval symbolism of the pelican. It is a symbol of the resurrection of our Lord and his sacrifice on the cross."

Ira and I both knew that the dream presaged future events. Jesus' return and the ingathering of the chosen were imminent.

31

TORNADO PROPHECY

Revelation 16

I had a silver pen which came from the clinic. I was puzzled by it and wondered how I managed to acquire it. I recall being in a building and my focus shifted skyward. I noticed the sky began to change from the pervasive overcast into something very different. After having been transported outside, I saw the clouds begin to disappear until only traces remained. These morphed into messages from God. The sky had become clear. The first message was, "All Gentiles, he is the God of the Bible." The next message mirrored Revelation. There must have been trembling, and then the sky became white light with fibers running through it. I became unconscious.

My paper was returned. The book form in which I had presented it was the same book I had written for Jesus in spring 1986. It was returned to me and inside the front cover was a grade with a big letter 'A'. Inside the back were the remarks of seven reviewers.

I left and went home to read the paper. Inside was a passage from the Old Testament, and then a series of beautiful, color plates of Israel. There were beautiful photos of the Jordan Valley with passages describing its fertility. There *were photos of people, as well. The last two I saw were of people waiting for a flood. Down river other people were awaiting the flood. Then they were inundated.*

I went home after work. I had already eaten and was working on a project for a friend. All of a sudden, I felt a sensation in my head which I have come to associate with the Holy Mother. I turned in my chair and waited with expectant curiosity.

A loud, terrifying voice spoke to me with authority, *"I am the Archangel Michael. The Holy Mother would speak with you!"*

Immediately there shone a blindingly brilliant star in front of me. *"There will be a tornado next Monday. This is a warning to mankind."* I understood that this meant if humanity neglected to turn to God the consequences would be serious.

The following day I shared the experience with my co-workers and a few customers. I thought about contacting the media, but I didn't even know how to provide a context for the experience. Instead I told everyone I knew, and prayed God would forgive my inadequacy.

That evening I told my friends at Tai Chi class. One just laughed at me, "There's not a cloud in the sky!" It was an atypical day for April, nearly eighty degrees and very humid.

"I'm only telling you what I was told." said I, shrugging my shoulders.

Three of us collectively agreed to go to our favorite Chinese restaurant for dinner. I ate my favorite dish, garlic eggplant. We had a fantastic evening. After a casual meal we all arose to go, they to drive to their condominium about fifteen miles away, and I to walk to my house about three blocks away.

As soon as we left the restaurant, we heard the sirens screaming. The city was blasting a tornado warning. The next morning I learned that in our fifty square mile corner of the county two tornados had touched down on either side of a co-worker's hometown, a funnel cloud had passed over another friend's house, and another had touched down in a community between the two. When I went to work on Tuesday, one of our customers walked in, and without even greeting us, she challenged, "Alright, what's going on?!"

I just chuckled.

Once again in the spring of 1994 Mary came to me with the purpose of giving a warning. Again, I was working on one of several projects. Again, I experienced the same "ring tone." Again, Michael announced her presence.

She said, *"There will be an earthquake on June 8. This will be a warning to all mankind."* The implication once again was if humanity neglected to turn to God the consequences would be serious.

I suppose it didn't seem to be a very significant revelation, as several hundred earthquakes occur somewhere on earth every day. This one, however, was significant. It was the largest earthquake in fifteen years. The epicenter was in Bolivia, but the tremors were felt as far away as Toronto, Canada!

32

DREAMS

Revelation 16

I *was in the storeroom. I walked back to a space behind and above the office. Jesus was seated there. I remarked at the musculature of his mouth. I approached him. He said, "You will drink with me."*

"I hope I am able."

Then I dreamed the Great Quake hit California. It shook everything from Texas all the way to Washington State and beyond. From high above California I saw the great cataclysm. It must have occurred during the dry season, as the landscape was arid brown and tan.

On another occasion…

From above a place east of Jerusalem I witnessed a great earthquake. The city was split, such that the land moved to the north and the south, separated along an east-west fault. The Jordan River was no longer running along its course.

Enter into My Rest

On another occasion...

While standing on a barren terrain, looking to my left I saw what appeared to be molten meteors pounding the earth. Their appearance was like volcanic bombs as large as small cars. The bombardment was unrelenting, and I felt great compassion for those who were suffering any kind of loss at that time.

On yet another occasion...

I was hovering above Lake Michigan, looking west. Chicago was under water up to the eighth or ninth floor of the Standard Oil Building. The peak of The Art Institute was completely submerged.

Our Divinity, layer 10

33

CHRIST'S RETURN

Revelation 19:11-13

A bright light shone in front of me. Jesus stood in light to the right. I told him, "I am so tired." He showed me I was in Spirit. Then there were two lights and I became one of them.

How can I describe what it is like to be lifted up out of mental, emotional and physical illness? On the one hand, while I existed in an unhealthy condition, it was impossible to see outside my circumstances. I suppressed so much, that I couldn't even feel the chronic physical pain. It felt like mud were circulating in the vascular system of my brain, and I choked on all my feelings. It was my emotions, interestingly enough, which led me out of the pit. Somewhere deep inside of me, I knew I could experience love, joy, and happiness.

On another occasion...

I was walking and stumbling up Golgotha. Lightning struck. There was a great flash of white light.

And on yet another occasion...

A man on a cross of light was wheeled into a room as if on a gurney. There were windows all around admitting brilliant light. There were several men seated around in a circle into the midst of which the cross was floating. This central portion was self-illuminated. One man in white robes stood to defend the man on the cross. The former was the advocate. The latter had my face.

Then a holographic image of Jesus, crowned with thorns, engulfed me, the observer. He was loving and reassuring. He told me, "You are not long for this world."

It's like climbing a steep mountain while you are dragging a dead dinosaur. At the top of the mountain beckons a light shining down. I knew I had to climb and was willing to invest for the long haul, because I knew there were no options. I wasn't giving up. At first, I thought I had no rope, no shoes, no harness, no skills, and no experience. But that changed.

One time I was in a classroom with numerous people, including Medicine Bear and David. It was light and airy. We were waiting for Jesus. Then he walked in through a door to my left.

Emotional boundaries are hard to establish and even harder to respect. It's like we're all swimming in the ocean, into which we're all dumping our sewage, chemical waste, drugs and garbage. It's very hard to swim away from that.

Enter into My Rest

On one occasion…

I had a dream of Jesus descending in flesh from Heaven. As he descended, he donned a red robe and with his hand reached up into his halo and pulled out a fir sapling with a white droplet on it. He continued descending as he handed the sapling to a man and told him to put it into his mouth.

Then there was the time when…

the Great One, Jesus, entered. The setting was a medieval castle of some height. His many children were waiting for him and onto his back a woman placed a long red cape with a rich ermine border. He accepted it willingly.

I struggled up that mountain. I had dropped that dead dinosaur a long time ago. And I learned that there was a top rope and Jesus was belaying me. He was not going to let me fall, and he was not going to let me fail.

Jesus appeared to me. He was wearing a pale blue robe with a white mantle.

The beating fist in my chest unclenched. It's funny how everything in this world is backward. Satan roams freely outside, while you are locked up in the jail of sin and ignorance.

Another time...

I dreamed I was outside looking up at the night sky. There was a pattern of golden stars shining brightly. I recall the stars were arranged in an oval with line-figures superimposed over them. The one most visible on the farthest left was the constellation Sagittarius. I was told that this was a sign that Our Lord's return was imminent.

One time...

I dreamed I was driving along a very busy inner-city highway. I was being chased. The traffic was too heavy and moving too slowly for me to escape my pursuer. I ran from my car toward the exit ramp, but the pursuer followed me on foot. As he was closing in, I saw two men dressed in white arrest and restrain him. I was so agitated I awoke.

I looked above my bed, and there I saw two white orbs of light flanking a red orb of light. The dream was an actual experience of two angelic beings restraining another being in order to protect me from attack.

I was taken up through death. I left my body and was taken into the tunnel. I was so aware that I was experiencing death that I was afraid. But I was aware that my love of God was far greater than my fear of death. So, with intense vibrating, I entered the tunnel. Then a vampire-like shadow figure spread out in front of me as if to block my passage. I commanded him to get out of my path in the name of Jesus Christ. Immediately he disappeared.

Enter into My Rest

He is the ultimate superhero. His supernatural abilities are greater than those of any demon that ever did befoul Creation. Imagine being able to vanquish the enemy with a word. And we are all drafted into the cause. Some of us fight by quilting. Others by preaching. Some by painting. Others by playing eight string classical guitar. The battle is real, the victory won. Don't think for a second this is some armchair battle here. Quite the contrary. It is a knockdown, drag-out fight, and the reward is the very substance of God for all eternity, for those who join the fray on the side of the Most High.

Our Divinity, layer 11

34

SATAN BOUND

Revelation 20:1-3

May 10th. My mother's birthday.

I was in some type of institutional building with cement stairs, blank walls, metal fire door and iron railings. A man whom I knew to be the resurrected Jesus appeared. He was tall, blond and wearing a robe. Three men came after him in order to kill him. He threw the leader into a cage and slammed a purple gate down through a space designed to receive it, thereby sealing the top 2/3 of the cage. Then he threw down a purple section of gate which filled the middle third of the bottom third of the cage entry. I took a piece of purple gate about the size of 1/9 the opening of the cage. I looked at the leader locked therein and challenged, "How do you like that?" There was so much force behind the slamming shut of the gates it was phenomenal! Jesus' gates were of painted, tubular iron, and my piece was made of painted, mini I-beams. His landed with a significant precision, mine fell pathetically to the bottom, but supported the others from below.

Mia, seeing what we had done, said, "There are orange gates we could use to lock up the others!" She went to retrieve them.

We had a demonic spirit living behind the wet bar under the slab of our relatively new house in New Jersey. The neighborhood was very old, the Bay Road houses having been built in the early 1800s. Once, when I was hoeing the beans in the garden, the hoe turned up a square nail of the type used during the Revolutionary War.

At first, we didn't know there was an evil spirit. How could we? It's not your run-of-the-mill, business-as-usual, kind of event. But it was our reality.

I remembered his face while I was in therapy. I had dreamed of the compartment with the lathe roll-up doorway behind the lift gate of the bar. Behind that door was something very dark. The trouble with darkness is one adjusts to it.

Several years later I learned that my mother, believing the evil something was active at 11:00 am, used to take the younger kids out of the house in order to protect them. She apparently believed it was active in the attic.

It was a horrible time in my life. That was the house where she would beat me bloody. With a belt. With rope. With a high-heeled shoe. With a hairbrush. She used to beat me with whatever object was near at hand. She was not strong enough to break the chain of abuse with which her father had killed her spirit. She was not strong enough to withstand the demons. She was not strong enough to conquer the addiction. In the end, evil was victorious.

Her father had abused her horribly. Finally, her mother had him locked up and lobotomized. It happened the night he was standing over her, ready to kill her. Mental illness tends to linger.

> ...for I, the Lord your God, am a jealous God, visiting the iniquity of the fathers on the children, on the third and fourth generations...
> (Exodus 20:5)

Enter into My Rest

Satan is like a stalking predator. He follows his prey. He observes his weaknesses. He beats down his victim. When his target finds inner strength, he strikes again. And again. And again. Like a cat with a mouse, Satan attacks and attacks and attacks, until the spirit dies. He steals the soul.

One day, when we older children arrived home from school, our mother was in a particularly disturbed state. Her eyes glowed like a rabid beast's. In her right hand she held a hammer, as she walked upstairs snarling and crying. She was going to kill herself. All three of us intuitively knew what she was going to do. We screamed and wailed hysterically, "NO, NO, NO, NO, NO!" And we just stood there impotently sobbing.

I don't know what we expected. Perhaps we thought she had succeeded. In spite of the many beatings, I still loved my mother dearly.

I don't know how long we stood there. Our sobs had turned into silence. I was numb.

After some time, she came quietly downstairs. The wild beast was gone. No longer tormented by the malevolence, she sulked her way into the kitchen, as we quietly returned to our usual after-school activities. We never spoke of it. And we certainly didn't tell Dad.

On August 11th she died. The coroner discovered the bruises on her chest, but I never learned of them until many years later. Dad and I were at dinner. It was my 40th birthday. I had visited our Upstate New York childhood home, where I remembered a time before the beatings had begun. When we moved to New Jersey, the beatings began, and steadily became increasingly bloody. "Why did she become so angry?"

And he told me. Of her father's violence. Of her struggle with alcoholism. Of her tortured inner life. I wanted to see her psychiatrist's notes, so that I might have an insight into my childhood experience. Did she hate me or was she just mentally ill? Would they ever tell me what prescription medicine she was taking? *Valley of the Dolls*, and all. Where were you when the lights went out? We were at the house of one of my dad's colleagues.

In 1999 I phoned the New Jersey State Coroner to report the chest beating, so that they might be able to close the cold case of my mother's death. Perhaps one day I shall be able to stitch the half of me that died with her back onto the half of me that lived.

NOW I SEE YOU FOR WHAT YOU ARE AND WHAT YOU TRIED TO DO TO ME! I REBUKE YOU IN THE NAME OF OUR LORD, JESUS CHRIST, THE SON OF THE LIVING GOD. GET THEE BEHIND ME IN THE NAME OF OUR LORD, JESUS CHRIST, SON OF THE LIVING GOD. Now I see you for what you really are. Now I see. You thought you would get me, but he is stronger than you. All power and authority in Heaven and Earth are his forever and ever. I rebuke you in the name of our Lord, Jesus Christ.

New Jersey devil, indeed.

35

DEATH

If anyone keeps my word he will never see death...
(John 8:51)

Revelation 20:12

One February night, I was lying in bed. I was having great difficulty sleeping. After several hours of tossing and turning, I felt a pressure on my forehead. I knew it was God and I surrendered to the experience. Then I felt pressure on my chest, and I surrendered to that. I arose out of my body. It was as if I were dreaming.

I rose up for what seemed an eternity. At one point I turned around and looked back at my bed. It was empty. I continued going up and once again turned around. There in my bed was a withered body curled up in a fetal position. I left through the crown of my head and passed through the house walls. Travelling feet first I entered the starry cosmos. As I travelled through the stars I felt them brush against me. It was glorious. Then I saw the Light at the end of the tunnel and began to chant, "God, I want to be with you!" And then I returned to my body.

Four days later, it happened again. About four in the morning, I was again in prayer. Suddenly I experienced the solidness and the vibrations in my heart and in my forehead, right temple and crown. Recognizing God's ring tone, I surrendered to the pressure once again. *The vibrations sounded as if I were filled with roaring, so loud was the deafening thunder. But for the knowledge of what I was experiencing, it would have been intolerable.*

I was taken up in Spirit. I felt Jesus' arms around my waist. We went up and up. Out of the corner of my right eye I viewed a sparkle of intense light. Recognizing God's glory, I turned to go to the Light. As I turned, I said, "I want to be with you."

A loud voice told me, "You're not ready for this."

With that I returned to my body.

Death and being taken up in Spirit are very much alike. The pressure on the different parts of the chest and head, the sound of rustling feathers or roaring waters, floating and looking back at the body are all common experiences associated with the early stages of dying. If you can let go easily, there's no fear or suffering associated with the separation of the soul from the body. It's rather unpleasant for me to return to the mortal cage once I've tasted the freedom of the spiritual world. The body suffocates and gathers pain to itself. It's like a straitjacket prison.

Death is not painful, though the means of death might be so for some of us. Harold once told me that death can be fun. He would know! Anyway, once outside the body you begin to lose attachments. The more of these that are removed, the lighter and brighter you become.

There is no question that death has changed me. When I learned that God is, I became exceedingly grateful. Not because of anything he had done for me, though he has done a great many things for me, but because he is! I was thankful, too, for the opportunity to make amends for all the wrongs I'd done and for the all the bad attitudes I'd cultivated.

Death gave me a reason to live. Until then this culture was the only paradigm I had. And it didn't attract me. I wanted to be motivated by the same things as everybody else: money, pleasure, power. But none of these fulfilled me. All my experience of those things compounded the inner emptiness I already felt. When I experienced death, I had a reason to live, even if that were only to serve others for the love of God.

I've always done everything I ever wanted to do. Before God found me, I did many immoral things. After God found me, I resolved to be with him, whatever that took.

Then, one Thanksgiving weekend, *I was standing in front of a barn. Montana Ventana was standing with me before the door. He held up the key to the barn. It was an old skeleton key. "I have the key to the video store." He opened the barn, into which I was impelled. It was entirely black. I knew I was dying. I began to recite Hail Marys as I left my body. I felt a sensation like rustling feathers at my arms and sides. A fluttering sensation was happening in my ears. I tried to breathe, but I became aware that it was an unnecessary activity. So I stopped breathing. Then I began to rise up the tunnel of light that I knew awaited me. After having ascended some distance I heard a woman scream. I had been given volitional control of the dying process, so I contemplated how I would proceed. I knew back in the world was someone who would soon be in need of assistance which I would be able to give. I returned to my body. As I descended, I saw Our Lady standing on my right.*

The next morning, I had an appointment to have a live blood analysis with a good friend. He put my blood under the microscope and, Holy Cow!

were there a lot of bacteria floating around in there! My blood was swimming with bacteria, coccoid as well as bacilliform.

"That would explain the ventricular arrhythmia just three days ago!"

I have low blood pressure to begin with, and clearly the bacterial blood infection was putting my body into a coma. Jeff recommended a shopping list of herbs, supplements, and other nutrients to help my body's immune system overcome the infections. My first thought was an overwhelming, *"We'll see about that!"*

But then I came to my senses and bought every product he'd recommended to me. It was going to cost me dearly, but I was going to get well so that I could assist the unknown person in need.

36

LAZARUS

...he who believes in me, the works that I do, he will do also...
(John 14:12)

Revelation 20:12

"I DON'T HAVE TIME FOR THIS!"

Medicine Bear had just phoned me. Joy's son had just hung himself.

Ira returned from his delivery. He worked part-time as an orderly at the local hospital. I told him about Lazarre hanging himself.

Miraculously, Lazarre's girlfriend felt an intuition to return to Joy's house after their argument. Equally miraculously Lazarre's brother, Jumeau, went to Joy's house, as well. Neither of them lived there, where Lazarre had hung himself.

His girlfriend found Lazarre's lifeless body hanging in the basement. She was too small to hoist his body up in her attempt to loosen the rope around his neck. Jumeau, though, was a muscular construction worker. He raced downstairs and rescued his brother's body from the makeshift scaffold while she phoned 911. When he had Lazarre's body down, he performed CPR. His body had become cold. By the time they got his body to the hospital, Jumeau and the medics had Lazarre's heart beating again.

Jumeau phoned Joy at school where she worked. Joy phoned Medicine Bear, who phoned me. That was about 4:30 p.m. "John, Lazarre just hung himself. I'm on my way to the hospital now. Joy's a wreck."

"Do you think it would be any good for me to come?"

"It looks bad. Do what you think is right."

"I can't come now. Ira is out on a delivery and I'm the only one here."

When he returned from the delivery, Ira didn't react to the story. He'd seen it before. I asked him, "Does this happen often? People hang themselves and then come back?"

"Yeah, about six a year."

"In this county?"

"In this hospital!"

I asked him, "Do they live?"

"Yeah, but only about twelve to thirty-six hours. The trauma to the brain takes over and then they die."

I was the manager of our store. A major highway reconstruction project was destroying our business. As it was, I was running around like a chicken with its head cut off. I was at my wit's end. My schedule was crazy, what with meetings with the city, the ad hoc business owners' organization, the Chamber of Commerce, not to mention the regular activities of running a business. Now this. I literally did not have time.

So, I prayed, *"Dear Lord, I don't know how to pray about this."* I couldn't judge Lazarre's action. How was I to know if this wasn't God's way of calling Lazarre home to himself? I didn't. *"God, I don't even know how to pray about this. Teach me what to pray."*

Enter into My Rest

I sat and listened. And it came to me. *"Lord, please let Lazarre live long enough to know the Joy, Peace, and Love which result from a relationship with you."* I prayed it over and over and over again. Having failed to ask Medicine Bear to which hospital they had taken Lazarre, all I could do was pray and wait and pace the floor.

I've known Lazarre since he was six. Cute kid. Mischievous. Used to work his cuteness to his advantage. Natural born salesman, like his father. His dad is Sicilian, and his mom the most beautiful walnut-skinned, African American. This causes their children unimaginable problems inasmuch as bigotry is alive and well and living in white, middle-class towns all over America.

Once, Lazarre and I collaborated on a school mask project. We used his face to construct a copy of King Tut's funerary mask. That was great fun. When he was fourteen, we went to see my friend, Dale, compete in a kick-boxing tournament. It was a very rough crowd. Everyone had to go through the x-ray machine. Everyone was frisked. The folks around us were yelling and screaming, farting and drinking. It was nothing like what I had expected. There were more fights in the bleachers than in the ring! My concerns were relieved when Lazarre called out to several men, Jumeau's friends whom he saw there. He wasn't the least bit uncomfortable!

Finally, Medicine Bear phoned.

"I'm here in emergency. Joy and Jumeau are here."

"Where are you?"

"Northern Peoples Hospital."

"Do you think it would do any good for me to come?"

"You have to do what you think is right. It looks bad, John. Real bad."

"I'm coming." I told Ira I was leaving and left him in charge. The hospital was only seven minutes away. When I arrived, I walked right into the ER. Medicine Bear was there.

"Joy and Jumeau are in there," she said, pointing me in the right direction.

I walked into the surgery. I saw Joy's face filled with unbearable despair. I hope never to see that kind of despair on another human face as long as I live.

Joy and Jumeau were working over the body, the one forgiving and encouraging, the other cajoling and petitioning as if will alone were sufficient to restore Lazarre to wholeness. Lazarre was hooked up to a ventilator so he could breathe, as the damage to his trachea was significant. The blood was siphoned off lest it fill his lungs and suffocate him. Adjacent the gurney was the heart monitor. Lazarre was in a coma. He was covered with a thin white sheet.

I held Lazarre's cool big toe with my right hand and embraced Joy with my left. And I prayed, *"Dear Lord, bring him back long enough that he will know the joy, peace and love which come with a relationship with you."* I prayed for guidance. I prayed for wisdom. I prayed for the healing of the family. I prayed to Lazarre to forgive himself for what he'd so violently done to his body.

Periodically I shifted from Lazarre's right to his left foot. As I held the feet, his body temperature had noticeably elevated. We were all sobbing over the tragedy. I could feel the Lord and Mother Mary grieving with us. They had so much sorrow over the suicide attempt. I prayed to them directly, *"Please, Lord, let Lazarre live long enough to know the joy, peace and love that come with a relationship with you."*

Above the bed appeared a golden cross, broad and thick, and bathed in light. It was the Protestant cross of the Risen Lord, rather than the Catholic crucifix. It remained above the gurney for some time. And I continued praying, *"Lord...joy, peace and love...in a relationship with you."*

After some forty-five agonizing minutes, the Lord spoke to me. *"He'll be okay."*

I knew in my heart I had heard the voice of God say, *"He'll be okay."*

I turned to Joy and whispered, "He'll be okay." She turned to those present and said, "John said, 'He'll be okay.'"

"There's nothing else I can do here." I embraced Jumeau and Joy in turn and took my leave. I raced home and phoned everyone who might have even the slightest inclination to pray. I asked each to pray as God inspired her or him, and I asked for prayers of comfort for the family. And then I continued to pray until exhaustion took me. I don't even remember going to bed.

The next day, Saturday, I had to work the store alone. I waited for the inevitable phone call. Ira had assured me that the people who can be revived after hanging generally suffer a seriously compromised condition during their brief resuscitation before the brain trauma takes over. So I interpreted the Lord's words, *"He'll be okay."* to mean he would be physically alive but brain dead, or he would be severely mentally handicapped, or he would have suffered some irrevocable brain damage. I was not prepared for what happened.

Medicine Bear phoned me at 10:00am. "I just talked to Joy. Last night at 10:30pm Lazarre came out of the coma. They moved him to ICU where he is apparently doing fine."

I broke down and wept uncontrollably. I praised God for having such mercy as to allow Joy not only to hear her son's voice again, but to have him restored whole and intact. Such awesome grace! I praised the Lord and thanked him all day!

I went to the hospital promptly after work. What I found can only be described as a three-ring circus. All of Lazarre's friends and family were camped in various places on ICU. I went into his room to find him eating burgers and fries and drinking soda! Barely twenty-four hours earlier, he had been comatose, hemorrhaging from the throat, struggling for breath. Now he was having a party with his friends! I leaned over to kiss his cheek. There wasn't even as much as a bruise on his throat!

I found Joy, who filled in the details. The neurologist had come in the morning to scan his brain for damage. He took one look at Lazarre and said, "You don't need this," and he walked out of the room.

We learned later the entire hospital nursing staff had been praying for Lazarre that night. I praised God in my heart for those women in the hospital.

I shared the fantastic news via e-mail with a friend:

Sweet Brother in Christ,

I visited Lazarre on Monday. He is now on the monitored care floor of the hospital. He is completely off everything. No meds. No machines. No monitors (of the mechanical kind!). He and I spoke briefly.

I was debriefing with one of my Christian customers. One thing which both she and I agreed upon was an opportunity to forgive myself the anger and arrogance which led me into attempting suicide many decades prior thereto. I saw in the forlorn faces of the bereaved brother and mother the faces of my loved ones whom God chose to spare the experience of losing me (for reasons of his own...).

I also brought up the chance circumstances which led ultimately to Lazarre's restoration to life. For example, if his brother hadn't, incidentally, unexpectedly gone to his parents' instead of his own house, where his brother/roommate had, incidentally, chosen to hang himself, no one would have been there to take down the body. The short version of the story is that all of the events in our individual lives led up to the moment whereby we were able to pray in that moment, collectively and individually. And God, clearly having a purpose beyond edifying our individual and collective egos, chose to restore Lazarre, in all ways, to an apparently normal human experience. All our individual and collective suffering became meaningful and useful to God in that moment, as, of course, became all our goodness, good intentions, good experience, knowledge, skill, and so on.

I am reminded of the millennia of preparation for Jesus, and the awesome profundity of meaning which his resurrection gave to the suffering of fallen humanity. I am reminded of the continuing forgiveness and redemption which that pivotal human experience afforded all of us who love him. I have never wept so hard, not so much for myself, though also for myself, as for the opportunity of Lazarre's mother to speak to her most beloved child yet one more time. I wept for the joy of a second chance for not one, but two prodigal sons, to return to fellowship with their heavenly Father.

I am keenly aware how ill-equipped I am to comprehend God's choices for my life at any given moment. I am also keenly aware how arrogant and angry I have been in my life. Having been utterly eviscerated, I tremble in awe (uncontrollably) before our Majestic, Omnipotent Lord. Let us all glorify him with all we think, say, and do.

Love, eternally, in him,

And so, I closed the email. I wept for weeks. I couldn't stop the flow of tears. I was so in awe of God, I told everyone with whom I came into contact. Everyone in church took pity on me, apparently assuming I'd just experienced some great, convicting transformation. Poor miserable sinner. Eat another cookie. Little did they know I had witnessed the Lord's majesty firsthand!

Our Divinity, layer 12

37

SISTER STORY

Revelation 20:12

After having been jerked around by grief, anger and denial, I was grateful when I became numb about 11pm that night. The cortisol levels in my blood were too high for me to sleep, but at least the emotions had calmed down. I slept only two hours before waking.

I did what I usually do when I awaken in the middle of the night: I prayed. As I lay there, I saw my heart open like a trumpet flower made of white light through which the Divine Presence was flowing in and out simultaneously. On the other end of this flow was the Throne of Glory with blinding rays of light streaming forth from it. Before the Throne was my sister.

And she was laughing! Her face shone with exuberant joy, as she looked over her shoulder to make sure I was seeing this.

Then her life review began. As I looked on, I saw the memories of her life flash before my mind. One in particular stood out above and beyond all the rest.

Several years ago, a forest fire threatened the west side of Flagstaff, near Mars Hill. The authorities had issued a mandatory evacuation order. Violators

Enter into My Rest

would be arrested and thrown in jail. As she worked as the dispatcher for the gas company, my sister knew about the order when it was issued. Even the crews were banned from going into the evacuation zone. But her little Shih Tzu, Buddy, was at home. She didn't care a hoot about the property or the possessions, but she wouldn't lose that dog.

Being a dutiful and responsible employee, she waited until it was lunch time to execute her plan. As she had immediate access to the fire situation, she knew that there was a window of opportunity to get her dog, and she took it.

Everything was going perfectly until she came to the intersection of Route 66 and Highway 17 by the Barnes and Noble. The police had erected a barricade, and plead as she might, they wouldn't let her pass. So, she turned away...

Anyone who knows my sister knows she was determined when she put her mind to something. This time was no different. Having driven home from work every day for years on end, she knew all the back streets, alleyways, and bypasses, as Flagstaff, being a tourist and college town, often has frustrating traffic jams. And she knew a little barrio behind the Furniture Barn, in which the roads were still unpaved. The authorities hadn't bothered to barricade anyone there. So, she plotted...

Furtively she drove on the dirt road that parallels the railroad tracks. She had driven the road often enough, so she knew where it emerged. She drove especially slowly, so as not to raise any telltale dust. Finally, she came to the Maverik, where the roads once again were paved.

There, driving eastbound on Route 66, was a squad car. She froze. She ducked below the level of the dashboard, only daring to peer out after sufficient time had elapsed. When she saw that he hadn't seen her, knowing she had a quarter-mile dash to the entrance to her subdivision and knowing there was no other way home except Route 66, she shot out and raced home as fast as she could. She rounded the corner of Union Pacific, pressed the garage door opener, shot in, and closed the door behind her.

She hid on the off chance that the policeman had seen her in his rear-view mirror and had turned around. She kept Buddy silent as she peered cautiously out her window. Sure enough, the squad car was coming directly to her house, looking for the car that had gotten by him. He drove slowly past while she hid. God stealthed my sister!

She waited long enough for the policeman to have turned onto a different road, grabbed Buddy, got in her car, and raced out of the subdivision. She turned east onto Route 66 and took off to return to work.

I asked her, "How did you get past the blockade?"

She replied, "I just drove around it."

I said, "My hero!"

And she cautioned, "Don't tell Dad!" She never wanted me to share anything she thought might upset him!

The fire consumed a substantial parcel of forest south of Route 66 and elsewhere in the area, but my sister's subdivision was spared.

Some eighteen years prior thereto, God took my sister up in Spirit and showed her what her future would be. She told me it was so liberating to be out of her body, as she was so light and agile in Spirit. Then she was thrust back into her fleshly body. It was so unwieldy and slow.

Our butterfly has flown, and I know she is as joyful as can be!

Jesus is my teacher, but with my sister at his side, a great big part of me is there now, too.

Enter into My Rest

38

ANGEL OF DEATH

Revelation 20:14

In 2017, I was dying of a tick-borne illness contracted while on a rock-climbing adventure. I had lost a tremendous amount of weight, was weak, and in tremendous pain. Walking was difficult.

One night the Holy Mother was standing by me. She was dressed in black. Radiance surrounded her. I knew why she was there. She showed no emotion whatsoever. She was there to fulfill a mission.

I was literally dead tired, so the objective reality of my imminent death held a certain welcome appeal. I've always lived intentionally, and in such a way so as not to have regrets. I've tried to live with the awareness of all my relationships. And, having chosen service to humanity for the love of God as my life expression, there were no tears at the prospect of a much-needed vacation. But there were all those teachings, given to me by ancestors and angels, which had not yet been made public.

So, I turned from the Mother and talked to the space to my right and above, addressing the Almighty, "I know you do not need me to get this information out. And you are God. I shall respect your will if this indeed is my time to leave. But it seems rather inefficient to have the ancestors and angels teach me all this information only to take me out."

And I heard, "You have been granted a reprieve." I knew then and there I had an assignment.

Nothing had ever humbled me so completely. It overwhelmed me that I'd been given an indefinite extension of life for the purpose of sharing these teachings. And it overwhelmed me to know how deeply God and the Holy Ones loved me. I'd never allowed people's love in, because my focus was on departing this life without any attachments. I wouldn't feel guilt, compulsion, or ownership. In the past I'd been aloof, cold, and even inhuman. But my past was no longer relevant. It had taken decades, but the Lord had changed my disdain for humanity into compassion.

Death continued to visit me at night for a period of about two weeks. One time, I was in the Spirit. The Holy Mother was above me and to my left. Jesus was above me and in front. Sai Baba was behind him. Round about them were myriad faces, including the Archangel Michael's. When Death came in his deep blackness, all of us pointed a finger at the space behind him, and with one voice said, "GET OUT! NOW!"

A number of times, a figure like the Grim Reaper dressed in the iconic hooded black robe came to me. I was alone on these occasions, but the command to "GET OUT!" was heeded. On one occasion, I told him in a conversational tone, "It's not my time!"

Like Jonah, who had such disdain for the Ninevites, I had disdained all humanity. One of my dearest friends once told me, "You need to tell the people what you've seen!"

"Who am I that anybody would listen to me? They already have Moses and Bharadwaj Rishi and Mohammad. Let them listen to them!" I was sarcastic, misanthropic and peevish. And like Jonah, I prayed that I might die. And just as he kept Jonah alive, God has kept me alive for his sake.

The result of the reprieve was a complete and permanent healing of my body. All the symptoms of the deadly disease are gone.

39

Jesus Comes to Dine

Revelation 21:3

I was meditating in bed, in deep theta yet conscious. Then Jesus filled me with the Light of God. I could see him inside me consciously. He was hugging me as he put his head on my breast. I made a confession to him. He gave absolution by way of a teaching. The light was so bright that I was physically blinded for a few minutes when the vision came to an end.

When Jesus said, "I will come in to him and sup with him" (Revelation 3:20), it was a literal statement of fact, not just a metaphor. There is a fusion of natures. And it is not limited to a select few to enjoy. It is for all who are willing.

When it happens, you are filled with his love, peace and joy. You will experience indescribable pleasure. You will know and be known.

Enter into My Rest

40

SPIRITUAL MIDWIFE

Revelation 21:4-7

Grandfather David, the great Hopi chief, asked Harold to take over his function as Spiritual Midwife. Harold would have been ideal for the job. And even though he had Indian blood, Harold discreetly and graciously declined because he was not Hopi.

Once I asked Harold, "What does a spiritual midwife do?"

He stated, "Just as a midwife assists in the delivery of babies into this world, a spiritual midwife assists in the delivery of the person into the spirit world." I had no clue what these words meant, but the metaphor was tangible enough.

Medicine Bear and I had been accustomed to meet every summer to celebrate her birthday. We always enjoyed spending time together. This year we met at the Grand Geneva for brunch. She was radiant, as always. Mostly we caught up on mutual friends and her children and grandchildren. I shared my research with her. She was always encouraging.

When it was time to say goodbye, we lingered. The Spirit told me this would be the last time I would see her. Inasmuch as I had had a life-

Our Divinity, layer 13

threatening illness in the previous year, it never occurred to me it would be she who would be going to the eternal picnic! So, I shined on her the most compassionate, soft, caring, affectionate and embracing smile possible. It was devastating, of course, to learn that it would not be I who would be passing over. It was even more devastating to learn that my dear friend, sister, and mentor was dying.

I spent many hours praying in the sweat lodge, in my bed, in meditation, and throughout the day. But I never knew how tired she was. The thirty years I'd known her, she was constantly attending political actions, tending her medicinal herbs, making medicines, teaching Cherokee wisdom, writing, and lecturing. And all the while she attended to the needs of her family and to her own spiritual cultivation. So, when the opportunity arose to go to rest, she took it.

Though I'd been blessed to experience death in many fashions on several occasions, something different happened when Medicine Bear took her leave. I was in my recliner praying for her. The transition was imperceptible as I allowed myself slowly to enter into a deep reverie. I found myself with Jesus and Mary in the spirit world, embracing Medicine Bear. Jesus was on my right; Mary was on my left.

And there we four were in the purest White Light. Medicine Bear was radiant and happier than I'd ever seen her. She was wearing a Buffalo Calf crown of pure white light. All was light, her garments, her skin, and we who were with her. She apologized to me. And then she was gone.

After her departure, I remained in that embrace with Mary and Jesus, but for only a short while. Then I slowly returned to my body. I had just become a spiritual doula.

41

NEW JERUSALEM

Revelation 21:10-21

I asked the angel, "When will these things happen?"

"In a time, times and a half."

"What does that mean?"

"What did the prophet Daniel say?"

"'From the time they set up the abomination of desolation 1,290 days' and 'how blessed is the one who attains to the 1,335 days'."

The angel asked, "What does that mean?"

"I have no idea. You tell me."

"How does John interpret Daniel?"

"Well, the 1,290 days are thirty days greater than forty-two months of thirty days each, and the 1,335 days are seventy-five days, or two and a half times thirty days, greater than forty-two months." I was full of myself for having perceived that!

The angel asked, "What was John trying to communicate?"

"Apparently he was drawing attention to the forty-two months of thirty days each."

Enter into My Rest

"Exactly! And what else?"

"That the three and a half years or 1,260 days also refer to these forty-two months."

"Correct."

"So, the forty-two months are about the process of becoming, the result of which is the return to the Garden of Eden."

"And thus is humankind perfected. It is equivalent to the arrival in the Promised Land, the coming of Messiah, or the ingathering of the exiles. It is the metaphor that Matthew encoded in Jesus' genealogy. What did God say to Abram? 'Go to yourself!' And in time he showed Abraham the coming of the Messiah."

Once again, the angels showed me the great cube called New Jerusalem. It collapsed into the Holy of Holies. This in turn was reduced to the tablets stacked one atop the other and placed inside the Ark of the Covenant, where the Creator is met face to face.

And there I was, a tiny octahedron of Light in the midst of the rose garden, blissing out in the Spiritual Light of God. All was as it should be and there was peace.

Instantly my mind exploded into the vision of the Cosmic Cube of Space. Even the constellations praise the Glory of God. The Lion, the Bull, the Eagle, and the Man define the four sides, like a cosmic cherub guarding the entrance to Eden. We were not so much exiled from the Garden as we exiled ourselves. The story was there before our eyes all along.

I swooned because of the majestic headiness of it all.

And the angel asked me, "Now do you get it?"

And I slid into the rosy light that separates the Creation from the non-created One, floating, conscious of the all, but not caring to analyze or examine it. And I found myself with myriad others standing on the eastern shore of the Jordan River where John had baptized Jesus, with the word 'nitzabim,' 'You are standing', blazoned on the fabric of the space-time continuum before us. This time I shall reach the other side.

Our Divinity, layer 14

42

IN THE GARDEN

On Saturday, June 23, 2007, I died. Jesus brought me up to the threshold of Heaven. In the distance, which was apparently to the west, was the Glory of God! Knowing I was home for good, I began screaming with absolute joy. I was allowed to run unfettered into God's Glory, as Jesus walked to his next appointment.

In my twenties, my spirituality was very superficial. Instead of his Presence, I felt only emptiness. I ate all the right foods. I breathed in all the correct rhythms. I practiced walking with awareness. I practiced mindfulness. I didn't speak ill of or to another human being. I always deferred to the will of others. I wanted to be so gentle that neither animals nor children feared me. I practiced every discipline, including fasting, praying without ceasing, and self-denial. I ate no sugar, salt, fat, or animal flesh. I drank alcoholic beverages on no occasion except Pesach, and then only wine. I exhorted those around me to live, love, and laugh. I served the homeless and the hungry with a vengeance. I practiced charity and fairness. I even exercised correctly and consciously. I acted as I imagined one would act in his Presence. I struggled to arrange my environs, so that I might have peace and harmony.

Enter into My Rest

And all the while, I was devoid of joy, love, and peace. On the outside, I was calm, kind, and healthy. Inside, however, was a cauldron of seething confusion. I lacked happiness altogether. I lived a dissatisfied, unpleasant, humorless life. I couldn't feel pleasure. I was as rigid as a board. I was a hollow shell of a man. But all that has changed.

In the beginning, all I wanted was the power of God, so that I might do whatever I wanted to do. Now all I want is to do God's will.

We were created only a little lower than God. Sometimes we fail to grasp the implications of our choices and our words. We're closer to the edge of Creation than selvage on broadcloth. If we fail to consult God in our prayers and our choices, the resultant fabric will be inharmonious with God's design.

Miracles are the norm for human beings, because we were created only a little lower than God. These are not the exception to the rule. Would a God who gave an ant the ability to carry something hundreds of times greater than its own body weight neglect to bless us, too?

It takes great wisdom to abide in God's Presence. Thankfully, he knows our hearts.

There I stand in the primeval forest, unchanged since the dawn of Creation. The 200-foot-tall trees reach up to Heaven in praise as diffuse light filters through the canopy. It is so silent here. Sounds generated hundreds of yards away seem as if they came from right next door. Ferns, bear grass, and Oregon grape carpet the forest floor. Huckleberry bushes abound. There is no one else around. The collective memory of ten thousand years of uninterrupted existence fills every atom of air, earth, and water, so that merely being is transcendent.

The great-grandmother trees stand upslope, watching over their progeny who populate the mountains all the way to the pristine river below. The deer and the bear and those of us fortunate enough to be here share this space with each other in balanced harmony. Here is a perfect ecology of existence. It is as if God had never left.

And then I was in a small room in which there was a solid oak desk, atop which was my typewriter, and around which were shelves stuffed with books. I had arrived home.

I stand in the midst of a perfect, octahedral crystal of adamantine light, whiter than the center of the sun. The consciousness of God crowds out all confusion. All pain is eradicated. Here is only the fullness of God's love and the awareness of eternity.

I turn around in search of the source of the light. There behind me is a magnificent throne in which the Holy One is seated. The light emanating from him is so brilliant I cannot see his face. In my mind, I say, "Just checking."

He is still.

Enter into My Rest

Our Divinity, layer 15

AFTERWORD

And remember all the journey that the Lord your God
led you on in the desert, in order to afflict you,
so that he might test you, to know what was in your heart...
(Deuteronomy 8:2)

LEKH LEKHA

"Come to yourself!" Genesis 12:1

Before the beginning the Creator formulated a plan by which those who had lost their way might find it. When God commanded Abram to depart from Chaldea, it set a ball rolling. Matthew interpreted that Jesus was the culmination of that process.

It is the process whereby we become receptive to Truth. And we can't do that from our recliners! Rather than reading about it, rip these pages from the book. Pin one page to the west wall, another to the north, another to the east, and another to the south. Pin one on the ceiling. Lay a page on the floor and sit on it. And then allow the answers, guidance, and wisdom to come in.

As I said early on, the magic interests me very little, *per se*. But if by sharing these stories I was able to attract your attention, then they will have served a useful purpose. I have chosen these stories to demonstrate that there is more to this world than meets the eye. Humanity is on the threshold of a significant revolution in consciousness. I wrote this material more or less as a primer for those who will be born some five or six generations from now. At that time all of these types of experience will be commonplace. After all, Joel prophesied such things nearly three millennia ago:

> *...and I shall pour out my spirit on all flesh, and your sons and daughters will prophesy, your old men will dream dreams, and your young men will see visions...* (Joel 3:1 [2:28])

As Jesus predicted,

> *"The one believing in me will do the works that I do, and even greater works than these..."* (John 14:12)

If there are lessons to be learned from these stories, the following are perhaps most important to me:

1. That which we call God, the Creator, or the Great White Spirit IS. Learning how that Being operates is necessary for enjoying the greatest possible earthly experience.

2. We are on a journey to wholeness, whether we want to do that or not, whether we are willing to do that or not, and whether we are aware of it or not. It's called life. Whether we come cooperatively or whether we come kicking and screaming is our choice.

3. The length of the Jerusalem Temple according to the evidence in Tractate Middot was the radius of the earth divided by 42,000 using the cubit discovered by Asher Kaufman.

4. The length of the Jerusalem Temple equaled one divine year, if we recognize that the radius of the earth represents the age of the Universe. This is based upon Rabbi Isaac of Acre's determination that the age of the Universe equaled 42,000 times one divine year, or 365,250 terrestrial years, or 15,340,500,000 years at the time of the creation of Adam.

5. The length of the Jerusalem Temple according to Tractate Middot was the polar circumference of the earth divided by 264,000 using Asher Kaufman's cubit.

6. Implicit in the Israelite concept of the Cosmos is the number 42. It is implicit in the Kabbalah and it is found in scripture. For example, at I Kings 7:15 it states "…a cord of twelve cubits compassed the second (pillar)."

   Using the ratio 22/7 for pi, this cubit equals 22/42. This ratio represents the twenty-two building blocks of creation divided by forty-two, the number of stages in the journey to perfection.

7. In both the Americas and the Middle East, there was the implicit understanding that time and space were related. We know this most easily in the Americas because the measure of the earth was computed in terms of the 260-day sacred Tzolkin, a measure used exclusively for calendrical calculations. The circumference of the earth equaled 2,700 times the 57m unit

times the Tzolkin. The resultant measure of earth's circumference was more accurate than any known in the European world until well into the 20th century.

In spite of my frequent use of the first-person singular pronoun, these stories are not about me. They are, in fact, parables in which I have been a participant and a witness. Though the stories are not about me, nevertheless the process has been mine. And I have learned many things along the way: compassion, love, patience, faithfulness, trust, peace, joy, humility, forgiveness, more forgiveness, and yet more forgiveness.

I learned that God is, that God provides, and that God hears our prayers. I've learned the hard way that life-threatening illness brings us closer to God, and that seemingly small peccadillos impact several spheres of relationships. I've been blessed to learn that sitting in the presence of a holy person is more impactful than decades of study. Above all else, I have learned that if we fail to grasp the lesson of forgiveness, all our learning based on analogical perception or deductive logic serves no useful purpose.

I don't encourage people to choose homelessness, or to live in the wilderness, *per se*. And wandering about as I did was very hard work. It cost me a lot, even though it might sound romantic or adventurous. What I do encourage is finding a teacher, walking humbly before the Creator, being charitable with our resources, and being fair in all our dealings with our fellow beings. Only then will our lives be successful.

Our Divinity, layer 16

About the Author

John Thomas Fuhler was called by the Lord in 1982. Never having read the Bible, he began to study the Gospels. The verse that spoke most loudly to him was Matthew 6:33, "Seek [you all] first the kingdom of God..." Not knowing what that meant, he set out in search of an answer.

For several years thereafter he was often homeless and always impoverished. At that time, he began studying the major religions of the world.

When the Lord sent him back to his hometown in the spring of 1988, John began serving humanity for the love of God, in the fields of health foods and alternative medicine.

Then one fateful day, again while reading the Bible, he read John 14:15, "If you all love me, you all will keep my commandments." That triggered an intense study of Christianity and Judaism, a study that continues to this day.

Websites: www.EnterIntoMyRest.com and www.JohnThomasFuhler.com
Email: eimr5780@gmail.com
Facebook: johnthomas.fuhler

ABOUT THE ARTIST

Lori Dobberstein has had a passion for creating in the visual arts since childhood, when she was deeply inspired at an early age by artists Michelangelo, Georgia O'Keefe, and Frida Kahlo. Her love for art led her to pursue a Bachelor of Fine Arts degree, where she explored her creativity through drawing, print-making, ceramic sculpture, and painting.

Although she was able to gain experience in many mediums, she realized that the shoulds and should nots taught in art school actually stifled her creativity and authentic expression. She found that following her intuition in the creative process gave her deep fulfillment and unending inspiration. The images that sprang from there she could not have thought up with the rational, left-brained mind; she had found her Soul's voice and tapped into the Mystery. Today she continues to follow the lead of her Creative Muse wherever it takes her, be it commissioned artwork, teaching Intentional Creativity, or other inspired projects.

Website: www.wingedwomanstudio.com